the house of the architect

the house of the architect

Anatxu Zabalbeascoa

RIZZOLI
NEW YORK

For Miguel

Many people have given their time and energy to aid me in the production of this book. I would like to express my particular thanks to Monica Gili for her advice, ideas, confidence, and support; to Elena Nachmanoff for her support and help in following up various projects; to Gustavo Gili for a series of especially important phone calls; to Elena Llobera and Alicia Martín Alcaide for tracking down a number of architects; to Sahara Conca for her support in the final editing and laying out of the book; to Jean-Pierre Estrampes and Rafael Vargas for their photographs; to all of the architects included here, and to their staffs, for their interest, attention, and efforts, and in particular to Miguel Ruano for reading and offering his comments on the final text.

First published in the United States of America in 1995 by
Rizzoli International Publications, Inc.
300 Park Avenue South, New York, NY 10010

First published in Spain in 1995 by
Editorial Gustavo Gili, S.A.

Library of Congress Cataloging-in-Publication Data

Zabalbeascoa, Anatxu.
    [Casa del arquitecto. English]
    The house of the architect / Anatxu Zabalbeascoa.
      p. cm.
    ISBN 0-8478-1873-X
    1. Architects—Homes and haunts. 2. Architect-designed
houses. I. Title.
  NA 7195.A7Z3313 1995
  728'.37'0922—dc20   94-39395
                                          CIP

Designed by Eulàlia Coma S.C.P.

Printed in Spain

Contents

THE HOUSE OF THE ARCHITECT

John Singer Sargent, *The Daughters of Edward Darley Boit*, 1882

Edgar Degas, *Interior*, 1868

Edward Hopper, *Eleven in the Morning*, 1926

Max Ernst, *Two Children Threatened by a Nightmare*, 1924

The Spanish writer Vicente Verdú sees the house as "between reality and desire, between body and dream, between what is possible and what remains to be longed for."[1] To him, a house is the least anyone should have, and yet, it could also become the most someone might possess. Both a shelter and a showcase, the house has a strange capacity to welcome dreams while sheltering necessities. It protects its inhabitants from the external milieu while it helps them to accommodate themselves in this same frightening environment. A puzzling, splendid, baroque home that makes one owner proud, could be another's nightmare. The naked walls of a modern building may become an inhospitable prison to one unable to judge the architectural value of spaces, who evaluates what he sees according to comparisons, or a superficial examination of the color, the feel, and the shiny bulk of the finishes.

Homes, like people, like any living organism, have an interior and an exterior that cohabit. The sheltering house which protects its inhabitants from adverse surroundings attracts so much attention and involves so much emotion that, just like the best fortified castles or the greatest cathedrals, it is sometimes forced to forget its original purpose and embrace a new representative function. The house can transform itself from a safe, private interior to an outward-turned advertisement, or beckoning—from protecting its inhabitants to helping them address the outside world. It is in this position of announcing or calling that the house has often been used by architects, many of whom have built their professions around it.

Domestic architecture has produced both physical examples and fields of intangible experimentation in new constructive theories, psychological conjectures, and sociological criteria. Among, and on, the house's walls, architects have built an empire of propositions that range from subterranean dwellings to buildings that scrape the sky. From storehouses in which the walls are invaded by past memories, to rigid architectures that isolate individuals; from floating homes and irrational fantasies to dream houses—architects have often found room for indulgence in domestic architecture, especially in designing their own homes.

Every house, regardless of its success, is the house of the architect, for only the architect knows what the house could have been and never will be, what views had to be sacrificed, or what materials were not approved. But what happens when architects inhabit their own houses? How much do they experiment? How do they live? *The House of the Architect* presents houses designed by thirty architects for their own use. It attempts to understand how each architect has turned a house into a home.

The Home

The eye is generally not as important when it comes to perceiving intimate spaces as the skin is. Architects, however, obstinate inhabitants of a visual universe, have paid little attention to all that escapes the eye.

Luís Fernández-Galiano [2]

Reconstruction of an Iron Age dwelling by W. Horn

Fernández-Galiano has described the double character of the home as both a thermal and a symbolic space. He has also pointed to an historical evolution that favored the functional essence of the house over the symbolic one: "Our contemporary fires heat without signifying: homes have gotten dumb."[3] On the other hand, historian Joseph Rykwert had previously written on the relationship between construction and procreation (they both have a constructive goal, they are both productive activities). So much construction, so many tangible goods attempt to deny the lightness, the ephemerality of time—and in the end, the evidence of death—as life's sine qua non.

Vitruvius attributed architecture's origins to the primitive hut, built to protect the fire, to maintain the heat that kept one warm. The first house was, therefore, built out of the need to protect a manmade fire. From that protected fire is derived a first definition of architecture as the construction of a home. It is understandable, then, that some languages give a familial sense to the word house (as in House of Kent, for example). It is possible that the idea of home, as a combination of house and family, goes back to the representation of a nuclear family associated with domestic architecture. Moreover, it is quite likely that a home could refer its inhabitants not only to a particular space but to a shared origin, to similar ideas, to a common history, and even to analogous thoughts and criteria: "Those sleeping on the same mattress are also bound to share the same opinion," as a popular Spanish saying goes. In the eighteenth century, French theorist Marc-Antoine Laugier imagined the first domestic dwellers cohabiting in the primitive hut—a small and intimate

space compared to today's larger homes with more efficient heating systems. A similar idea of the simple hut as the basic expression of the home was revisited in the mid-twentieth century by the Italians Aldo Rossi and Giancarlo de Carlo, and the Spaniards José Luís Fernández del Amo, Alejandro Herrero Ayllón, and Alejandro de la Sota, among others. These architects aimed to give people the pitched-roof houses that seemed natural to their cultures and habits. The houses were painted bright white, green, and orange, and became a type that was later to be called populist architecture.

The Enclosed Fire: The House

Architecture must have had a very simple origin in the primitive effort men made to protect themselves against violent weather changes, wild animals and human enemies.

Banister Fletcher[4]

If architecture is the shaping of space, calligraphy would be a shaping of ideas, and the physical values of each would imply limits, would supply boundaries necessary for defining concepts. The piece of land enclosed by the walls of a house is, as Le Corbusier pointed out, the extension of the individual's body—and it is only by depending exclusively on the body and mind that the individual can obtain the illusion of total freedom. The house is one's fortified body, one's armor. It is a mute and respectful confidant, a witness of whatever takes place in its interior, a warm lap, and yet a mysterious veil when seen from outside. It is this exterior aspect that has transformed the

David Hockney, *My Parents,* 1977

The first building according to Viollet-le-Duc

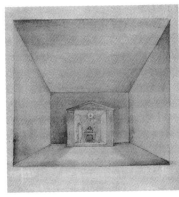

William Blake, *A Vision: The Poet's Inspiration,* c. 1819–20

The primitive hut of the abbé Laugier

Georg Friedrich Kersting, *Reader by Lamplight*, 1814

Adam sheltering from the rain according to Filerete

home from a mere shelter into a show-case, from a protective, intimate space, into one that has been forced open by social imposition. In this way, the house is transformed into a public face of its own complex, inhabited interior.

Faced with the impossibility of under-standing people's souls, occidental cul-tures have invented consolatory myths to make themselves stronger. The saying "the face mirrors the soul" could also be understood as "the house mirrors its inhabitants" (after all, the inhabitants are the soul of the house). For another popular saying, "tell me who your friends are and I will tell you who you are," the analogous assumption is that personalities can be interpreted based on the decoration and furnishings of a house. Aldo Rossi, in *A Scientific Autobiography*, spoke of the primitive hut as a second body, as an element that could be dressed or un-dressed according to climatological needs, and to agree with whatever changes the owner felt most convenient.[5]

Vitruvius's original idea of the protected fire is often used as a metaphor in this context of huts and lodgings, dens and lairs as the most elemental architecture, existing closest to one's body, as a third skin, after the epidermis and clothing. Among many others, Eugène Viollet-le-Duc supported these ideas when he compared the primitive hut with the skin of a snake. A century earlier, in 1753, abbé Marc-Antoine Laugier worked towards a simplification of architecture, researching the concept of the simple roof with two supporting pillars. According to him, all walls should be liberated from their struc-tural load and only supporting, free-standing columns should remain.[6]

This simplification of the home, including the abolition of ornament and a gain of spatial flexibility and fluidity, was one of the proposals that appeared in the model housing programs of the 1920s, estab-lished by the Bauhaus in Germany in an attempt to produce housing able to dig-nify human existence. Despite the original objectives, the houses remained mainly experimental. Georg Muche, designer of a model house under the supervision of Aldolf Meyer and Walter Gropius, and one of the fundamental ideologists in this research, declared that the best homes were useless when their inhabitants did not take advantage of new discoveries in materials, technology, spatial flow, and home appliances. To Muche, the home was an ideal enclosure, fundamental to maintaining the individual's mental and physical health.

Le Corbusier reinforced these ideas in his proposal of 1914 for the Maison Domino and of 1915 for the Villes Pilotis, in which ornament was also abolished and de-mocracy was sought. "If we remove from our minds and hearts old, already dead, domestic concepts, and take a new look at this issue from a more critical point of view, we will reach the 'Machine-House,' a mass produced house as beautiful as the tools and machinery that we live with."[7] Le Corbusier, who compared the house with a "machine for living in," combined these two proposals in some of his later designs, such as the Maison Citrohan and the Ville Contemporaine, in which he sought to apply his domestic principles to urban planning. He believed his domestic designs to be the unequiv-ocal cores of architectural organization. To him, the house was not only the family nucleus, but also a basic urban reduction, the first cell towards the building of a city.

In a theoretical program published in 1918, the German architect Bruno Taut had also anticipated the ideas developed by the Bauhaus. Like Gropius, Taut thought that cultural unity could only be achieved by means of a new building art form. He also felt that all forms of artistic representation should reinforce architecture just as in cathedrals, which throughout history have contained sculpture, painting, woodcarving, tapestries, embroidery, and even music among their slim and pointed walls. From there, Taut announced, "boundaries between crafts, sculpture and painting would eventually vanish and that, in the end, everything would be part of the architecture and, therefore, considered architecture."[8] According to Taut´s ideas, by becoming a container for the other arts, the house would acquire a showcase value in addition to its primitive, protective function.

Shelter and Emblem: The Home and the House

The house has a paradoxical quality in which it functions both as shelter and as advertisement, each with its own very different effect. While the house interior was originally intended to protect and comfort its inhabitants, the exterior soon acquired a more representative function that gradually surpassed the original protective intention. Walter Gropius strove to annul the difference between the interior and the exterior of the house in a series of studies called the total work of art. According to Gropius, the visual arts' uppermost aim should be to build, and therefore all arts should be mixed in architecture. Like Taut, Gropius sought a constructive solution in the homogeneity between interior and exterior spaces. To him, the interior and exterior of a building needed not only to correspond, but to mutually announce each other. His ideas precluded the possibility of the hiding wall, the veil of intimacy, the space to protect the fire, and the calling-announcing place. Cleanliness and clarity were to be imposed by the total work of art. To Gropius, reasoning was far more important than pride, and therefore either shelter or showcase needed to be sacrificed.

Bauhaus theorists maintained that lack of housing or neglected conditions could cause social revolts, unhappy citizens, and even vandalism and antisocial behavior. They believed that all individuals should have homes of their own, which would dignify their existence and make them free people. It was not long, however, before they realized that while the idea of owning a house was appealing to many people, the home most individuals preferred was not a model house, but rather a Swiss-like chalet made of stone or brick with a slate pitched roof.

Houses as Laboratories and Houses as Manifestos

For many architects, the house of a relative or friend is their first opportunity to freely design and manipulate space. As a consequence, the architect's domestic work is often a collection of built manifestos: the materialization of ideals. It is not strange, therefore, that many architects' names have been added to the history of architecture because of the

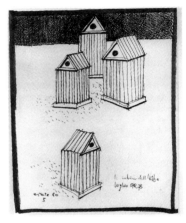

Aldo Rossi, cabins on Elba, 1975

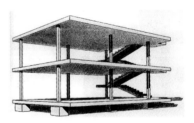

Le Corbusier, Maison Domino, 1914

Gerrit Rietveld, Schröder House,
Utrecht, Netherlands, 1924

construction of a particular house: G.T. Rietveld's Schröder House, Pierre Chareau's Maison de Verre, and Adalberto Libera's Villa Malaparte.

There are also family names sharing this same history, supported by their own homes. In commissioning their houses, these people commissioned further experiments in architecture. They acted both as clients and patrons of the arts. There are few instances in which clients rely blindly on the architect, and even fewer in which the resulting design is a masterpiece. In the rare cases when the designs are truly masterful, the homes have entered the history of modern architecture closely associated with the names of the owners, rather than the architects. Schnabel, Stoclet, Steiner, Mairea, Winslow, Farnsworth, Milá, Müller, Catasús, Schröder, Robie, and Kaufmann are some of the names that, together with kings, popes, and politicians, share a place of honor in the lists of historic architecture patrons.

After years of being visited and worshipped by architects, some houses have also been recognized as architectural manifestos, due to the unusual programs and new architectural concepts they introduced. Fallingwater (the Kaufmann House by Frank Lloyd Wright, located near Mill Run, Pennsylvania) integrated nature and dwelling in a very different way from the approach taken in another Kaufmann house (by Richard Neutra, built in California). The Schröder house, together with famous red-blue chair by Rietveld, is the main emblem of Dutch neoplasticism, just as many of the curves and mosaics of the art nouveau buildings built in Spain in the beginning of the twentieth century

refer to Antoni Gaudí's Milá House in Barcelona. The designers of these manifesto-homes have received international recognition, and often the veneration of younger architects. Many of these buildings have become museums or architectural pilgrimage places, not so much because of the history they house, but because they have become so emblematic of a particular period or style.

The House of the Architect

Sponsoring something involves betting strongly on that thing—having faith in its results. With this in mind, it is easy to understand the intimidation many architects face in designing their own homes. This intimidation is more a proof of humbleness than a sign of cowardice. Many professionals talk about the design and construction of their own homes as the most difficult exercise they have had to undertake. Some architects create never-ending homes, houses always under construction. The most existentialist architects point out that a home is never a space enclosed by four walls, but rather the mutual feeling of belonging its inhabitants are able to achieve. These architects leave domestic issues out of their architectural practices, stating that their work is not a protective task, nor a perpetuation of the family nucleus, but rather an issue of adaptation to the environment. It seems that the house of the architect is one that grows with him, transforming itself, learning, adapting itself to its inhabitants' changing needs, just like human skin does, and the feathers and furs of animals. This condition of unceasing construction clearly illustrates the organicist philosophy of Le Corbusier that defines the house as the extension of the body.

Designing a house has often been the catalyst that enables an architect to start a professional practice. It can often also reflect the architect's professional maturity. Carlos Jiménez's house in Houston illustrates the former, although as years have gone by, and many remodelings and additions have been made to the original house, it has also reflected his career's evolution. It has confirmed the type of precise formal language and simple volumetric spatial conception Jiménez is interested in. On the other hand, Frank Gehry's house in California, which had already achieved the status of a manifesto-house for many architects prior to its most recent remodeling, has perhaps now truly become this manifesto-house. By disappearing it has gained a utopian quality—it has achieved the degree of impossibility required for any manifesto to remain utopian. Meanwhile, Gehry the person, not the architect, enjoys larger spaces and the comforts of air conditioning in his new home.

Art history books divulge the name of the first known architect: Imhotep, the architect of the step pyramid of King Zoser at Saqqara, in old Egypt. Later, with the individual recognition of architects developed in Greco-Roman culture, many architects were able to add their names and works to the books of architectural history, although it is the patrons, with very different nationalities, intentions, and beliefs, who have more often been associated with famous and historic buildings. In both cases, almost nothing is known of the architect aside from his professional career. Even though they designed cath-edrals, funerary monuments, or palaces, architects in the past usually lived in ordinary houses that echoed the style of their village. Seldom did they research construction methods or designs in building their own homes. Very little indeed do we know of architects' personal lives compared with what we know about the lives of musicians, politicians, painters, and statesmen.

Until fairly recently, architects' houses have been a little-known field for architecture historians. Monticello, by Thomas Jefferson, is one of the first well-known examples of an architect's own home. Granted, Jefferson was also a statesman, a politician, one of the authors of the Declaration of Independence, and later the third president of the nation, all of which could be more significant reasons Jefferson's house is so widely known. In addition to Monticello, built in Virginia (1768–82), some other very significant buildings by Jefferson, such as the Virginia State Capitol in Richmond and the University of Virginia in Charlottes-ville, have enriched American architectural history. As George Washington's Secretary of State, Jefferson played a leading part in planning the new federal capitol in Washington from 1792 onwards. He deeply admired Roman law, and by extension he consciously absorb-ed the principles of Roman architecture that his buildings reveal.

Also inspired by ancient Rome, and considered one of the English Palladians, Lord Burlington designed his own London home, Chiswick House (c. 1730). Designed with the perfect symmetry of Palladio's Villa Rotonda of 1569 in Vicenza, Italy, the house of the British architect

Monticello, Thomas Jefferson's house, near Charlottesville, Virginia, 1768–82

Lord Burlington, Chiswick House, London, England

Horace Walpole, Strawberry Hill, Middlesex, England, 1748

Sir John Soane's house, London, England, 1812

Louis Sullivan, Guaranty Building, Buffalo, New York, 1894–96

Villa Hvitträsk, the home of Saarinen, Lindgren, and Gesellius near Helsinki, Finland, 1902

incorporated four chimneys, necessary for combating the London weather, in the shape of obelisks.

A few years before Monticello was built, the famous gothic revival mansion Strawberry Hill in Middlesex, England, by Horace Walpole, had more romantic than architectural value. Together with the follies of Sanderson Miller and James Stuart in British Worcestershire (1748 and 1758), and probably comparable to the Royal Pavilion erected in Brighton by John Nash (1815), the work of Walpole recovered Gothic elements to mask Georgian architecture. Walpole did not seek to evoke the principles and intentions originally associated with this type of architecture; his project was rather the result of a particular nostalgia for antiquity at the time.

A similar nostalgia was later evident in the design of well-known British architect Sir John Soane for his own London home of 1812. Rather than evoking the past, however, Soane absorbed it in order to design without neglecting or refusing any current architectural knowledge. He produced a very austere architecture for the exterior. As architect for the Bank of England (1788–1833), Soane had incorporated a series of caryatids as supporting columns for the central dome of the building. These sharply contrasted with the rest of the unornamented construction. In his London home, he segmented the arches and invoked an ornamental serenity similar to that of the Bank of England and other works. He used diverse architectural resources, particularly transparent elements and mirrors that gave the home the same sense of continuity he had achieved in his professional commis-

sions. The effects of light as well as his dome and mirror ideas in his house were later to inspire many other architects.

In 1890, the American architect Louis Sullivan, under whom Frank Lloyd Wright was to start his professional career in 1888, designed his summer residence in Ocean Springs, Mississippi. In that house, Sullivan showed his special ability to combine his organic vocabulary with the then-emerging technologies. The design and construction of this house took place simultaneously with the building of two of his most prominent works: the Wainwright Building (1890) and the Union Trust Building (1892–93), both in Saint Louis. Later works, such as the Guaranty Building (1894–96) in Buffalo, New York, would progressively develop Sullivan's approach to technology from a very personal organic perspective.

Near Helsinki, Finland, at the beginning of the century, the Villa Hvitträsk (1902) was an admired, ground-breaking effort to build a house that would function as a home-office. The story of this residence, which was designed by Finnish architects Saarinen, Lindgren, and Gesellius, also contains intriguing insights on power, aesthetics, human relationships, and architecture. Begun in 1893, the villa was intended to house the families and offices of the three architects. Perhaps because of the villa's proximity to and relationship with local wooden architecture, the house did not develop the architects' design aesthetics so much as it provided a location for their lives and families. Before construction was finished, Saarinen and Gesellius exchanged wives (or the wives exchanged husbands). The new Mrs. Saarinen, ex-Mrs. Gesellius, would later become the mother of another of the most important figures in the history of Finnish architecture, Eero Saarinen. The personal changes and agitated relationships, as well as Eliel Saarinen's independent entry in the competition for a new railway station in Helsinki, helped dissolve the professional partnership. Saarinen won the competition, departing from the vernacular architecture he used in his own home to embrace the Jugendstil that was, by then, flourishing in Europe.

Frank Lloyd Wright's ideas regarding domestic architecture remain widely known. In his prairie houses, early in his professional career, the architect explored the possibilities of new materials and construction methods. In his later California houses, Wright explored a new building system by using prefabricated concrete elements to build the block houses. In 1928, he coined the word Usonia to identify the egalitarian culture he hoped would someday exist in the United States. The widespread ownership of automobiles led to a new type of country-city, and Wright went so far as to design Broadacre City as a prototype, which, although it was never realized as such, greatly influenced Wright's designs for future projects. Constructions in this proposed plan were to integrate easily with nature, as did his contemporaneous designs for St. Mark's Tower (1929) and the "Capitol Journal" Newspaper Plant (1930). The first sketches for these projects show how Wright intended lightness where in traditional construction there is weight, such as in ceilings, and weight in usually light components, as in walls. The Johnson Wax Building in Racine, Wisconsin would be based on these principles. The Usonian houses designed for Broadacre City were designed as simple, warm spaces with very specific provisions for economy and comfort. A kitchen, a bedroom, and an open working place were the main spaces in these houses. Frank Lloyd Wright must be credited for the tight consistency between what he espoused and what he actually designed and built. His first house in Oak Park, Illinois, built in 1885, shares ideas and architectural concepts with his Guaranty Building in Buffalo, New York, started the same year, while he still worked with Louis Sullivan. Wright's later Taliesin residences, the first in Spring Green, Wisconsin in 1911, and the second in Scottsdale, Arizona in 1938, also speak of the diverse ideological and architectural phases Wright went through during his architectural career. Both Taliesin compounds adapt themselves to the natural environment as easily as does the Kaufmann House, Fallingwater (1935). Also, both of them integrate a professional work space into the living quarters, just as Wright proposed in his Usonian residences.

Antonin Raymond, one of Wright's assistants, built for himself the first-ever reinforced concrete house in Tokyo (1923). This North American architect of Czech origins had arrived in Tokyo four years earlier to supervise the construction of Wright's Imperial Hotel, which was also of reinforced concrete. Raymond's house in Tokyo exemplifies the use of reinforced concrete formally adapted to traditional Japanese wood construction. After the Second World War, the building material and technique imported by Raymond would become a primary feature of Japanese architecture.

Frank Lloyd Wright, house in Oak Park, Illinois, 1889

Frank Lloyd Wright, studio in Oak Park, Illinois, 1895

Frank Lloyd Wright, Taliesin I, Spring Green, Wisconsin, 1911

Frank Lloyd Wright, Taliesin West, Scottsdale, Arizona, 1938

Antonin Raymond, house in Tokyo, Japan, 1923

Eileen Gray, House E-1027, Roquebrune, France, 1926–29

Konstantin Melnikov's house, Moscow, Russia, 1927–29

Gunnar Asplund, summer house in Sorunda, Sweden, 1937

Alvar and Aino Aalto, summer residence in Muratsalo, Finland, 1953

Eileen Gray's E-1027 house, built in 1926–29 near Menton, France, was the first residence of this self-taught architect, as well as the first project in her very short list of architectural designs. A painter, and furniture and pattern designer, Gray was an example of the total artist. She produced a complete body of work that enabled her to deal with all types of domestic needs. Unlike the vast majority of architects who never get to build their own homes, Gray did it several times—as a matter of fact, her architectural production is limited to those examples. For Gray, architecture was a part-time occupation at a time when she was producing furniture designs which were to become part of the history of avant-garde furniture. Le Corbusier later invited Eileen Gray to collaborate in his Pavillon des Temps Nouveaux in the Paris Exposition of 1937. There, just as she had done throughout her career, Gray applied and reinterpreted modernist principles. In each of the homes she designed, the 1027, the Tempe a Pailla, Castellar house, and the apartment on Chateaubriand Street designed for a friend, Gray built very rational spaces and all the furniture that belonged to those spaces. It was an attempt to attain the total work of art that members of the Bauhaus had envisioned.

After Gray finished her first house in 1927, Konstantin Melnikov designed his own in Moscow. The Russian architect had designed a very dynamic Soviet pavilion for the Paris Universal Exposition of 1925. There, his design had been based on the intersection of deformed geometric volumes that forced visitors to follow a certain path through the building. Two years later, when he designed his own dwelling, he intersected two cylinders to obtain an unusual space whose floor plan was the infinite symbol of a reclined 8.

In Sweden, Gunnar Asplund's work was announcing an imposing return to classicism and to a romantic tradition that adapted itself to the vernacular landscape. By combining the simple volumes of the indigenous tradition with a revisited classicism, Asplund aimed to achieve a more authentic vernacular expression. His summer residence at Sorunda, near Stockholm (1937), reflects his profound respect and understanding for his own vernacular culture. Asplund's projects strongly influenced the first years of Alvar Aalto's professional development. Aalto later abandoned the vernacular architectural style to favor a more functionalist and pseudo-organic approach that helped him win first prize in the competition to design the Tuberculosis Sanatorium in Paimio in 1928. As architect and historian Kenneth Frampton pointed out,[9] Aalto's Paimio sanitorium also helped him develop constructive details inside the building at a time when he was starting the series production of his furniture designs. A relationship with local industry, in particular the Finnish wood industry can be appreciated in many of his works. In Villa Mairea (1938), one of Aalto's most celebrated projects, which he designed as a summer house in Noormarkku for his friend Maire Gullichsen, Aalto combined native woods with brickwork. The rustic interior and the exterior finishings unify the design. The structural use of wood, both in finishings and interior partitions and articulations, place Villa Mairea among Aalto's masterpieces, and it remains a significant statement in the history of functionalist-organic architecture. Aalto and his wife

Aino designed their own summer house and their studio in Finland. Both buildings are examples of Aalto's personal interpretation of the modern movement.

Arne Jacobsen was another of Asplund's admirers. Jacobsen's private house in Charlottenlund (1928) is one of the first examples of the Danish architect's progressive departure from the vernacular tradition toward an enhancement of modernist principles by means of employing new materials for old uses. Jacobsen's house had a reinforced concrete structure and a flat roof that was an important departure from the traditional pitched roofs he had been using until then. The plan featured a flexible interior partition system that allowed various spatial configurations. The slightly later home of M. Rothenborg (1931), also by Jacobsen, is a more developed product of a new architectural culture.

Walter Gropius's forced exile from Germany brought him to Harvard University where he was to become Chairman of the department of architecture. The house he built for himself in Lincoln, Massachusetts (1937) is an adaptation of Bauhaus architectural principles to a new cultural context and a foreign architecture. When historian Lewis Mumford visited Gropius in his new house in 1939, he quipped that Gropius's house was a new home for New England, for the new England of the new world.

Also exiled, but in California, Austrian architect Richard Neutra applied similar architectural principles to his domestic designs. The Kaufmann House, also known as the House in the Desert, is one of the most outstanding examples of his

sensitivity and subtlety. A very similar line was followed by Charles and Ray Eames when they designed their own home in Santa Monica (1949). Participating in a competition to design the home of the future organized by *Arts & Architecture* magazine, the Eames couple employed the new construction methods, materials, and techniques that industrial prefabrication offered. By using a metal structure, they achieved a beautifully fragile-looking house, in which light and the different effects it produced allowed a geometric and playful relationship between indoor and outdoor spaces.

Philip Johnson's Glass House in New Canaan, Connecticut (1949), pays homage to Mies van der Rohe's famous Farnsworth House (1945–50). In fact, when the construction was finished, Johnson wrote: "Many details of the house have been adopted directly from Mies's works: the way in which corners are treated, the relationship between columns and window frames and even the use of standardized sections and steel finishings achieve a strong and decorative sense Mies's Chicago buildings did have."[10] In Johnson's case, however, the exterior structure did not correspond to the interior structure with the same fidelity as Mies's designs. The manipulated perception of continuity between interior and exterior was to remain a feature of most of Johnson's later works.

American architect Buckminster Fuller designed the first version of his Dymaxion House (dynamism plus efficiency) in 1927, and by ten years later he had developed ten different models for a similar house that was to be mass produced. It was not, however, until 1946 that he built

Arne Jacobsen's house, Charlottenlund, Denmark, 1928

Walter Gropius, house in Lincoln, Massachusetts, 1937

Charles Eames, house in Santa Monica, California, 1949

Philip Johnson, Glass House in New Canaan, Connecticut, 1949

Buckminster Fuller, house in
Carbondale, Illinois, 1966

Jørn Utzon, house in Porto Petro,
Mallorca, 1971

the home generated by this experimentation. Of hexagonal floor plan, the house
was suspended from a central pole. It was
explained by Fuller as a mixture of North
American skyscraper and oriental pa-
goda. Fuller's own home in Carbondale,
Illinois was built using the speedy construction methods he defended. It had a
curious formal expression derived from
its mass-produced origin, yet it was simple, round, and unornamented. Because it
was prefabricated, it was probably not
intended to have the aesthetics of a finely-
crafted machine.

Among the most famous second homes
and summer residences is the house of
Danish architect Jørn Utzon on the Spanish island of Majorca, which in its composite simplicity reveals Utzon's magnificent opera house in Sydney, Australia.
Although the architectural strength of his
Majorcan house does not formally refer to
the opera house, the same skilled hand is
evident in both projects' fluid composition and easy volumes.

A local tale has emerged around Utzon's
Majorca house. In the Balearic Islands, a
soft local stone called Marés is cut into
cubes and baked in the sun to be used for
construction and other purposes. Utzon
was playing with sugar cubes one day in a
café near Valldemosa, when someone
asked what he was doing, and he replied
that he was designing his home. Utzon's
house in Porto Petro (1972) belongs to a
class of buildings that best define the
modern movement. The house commun-
icates Utzon's personal respect for the
architectural context in which it is built,
thanks to the simplicity of its volume and
the use of local building material. This
house has the exquisite serenity and

discreet perfection of a building designed
with an appropriate scale and the proper
materials.

The Vanna Venturi House (1964) in Chest-
nut Hill, Pennsylvania is a building with
radically different values, reflecting the
complex and contradictory architectural
principles of Robert Venturi. Venturi's
mother lives in this asymmetrical space in
which the noncorresponding interior and
exterior protect her privacy in the rig-
orous and primitive sense of traditional
domestic architecture. The Vanna Venturi
House has become a manifesto-house as
a proponent of the monumentality that
was lost with modernism—a defender of
the ideas Charles Jencks later called
postmodern.

Frank Gehry's home in Santa Monica,
California (1978–93) marked the beginning of a remarkable architectural flourishing in the Los Angeles area. It was
acclaimed and admired for its daring
construction, its volumetric composition,
and for a unique use of industrial materials. According to Gehry, architecture
should be free of the associations normally made between certain materials
and specific statuses, avoiding references and classifications. Many architects cannot forgive Gehry's recent
extension to the house, accusing him of
having demolished a monument. Deny-
ing Gehry the right to remodel the older
home he originally altered in 1978 is as
absurd as pretending to maintain the
primitive hut that Abbé Laugier wrote
about as the purest, and therefore the
only possible architectural form. Gehry's
house in Santa Monica is, above any-
thing else, his own house, and with
all experimentations and manifestos

aside, it is he who must comfortably live in it.

During the design process, the house of the architect can play a dual role both as domicile and laboratory for researching design issues—whether this consists of searching the core of an old building, camouflaging an addition inside an existing construction, or changing the typology of a building. Rare is the professional architect whose public architecture is radically different from his private one. The process of designing a personal house can help sort the tangle of design aesthetics, philosophies, methods, and attitudes many architects contend with in their commissioned work. The visible work of commissioned projects is just a small part of the architect's production potential. Just as Goya's *Goyescas* series reflects his personal desire to portray the truths of his society, so it is that the most outstanding works, the most intimate designs, the true *Caprichos*[11] are found in the home. This is why it is so compelling to glimpse the private realms of those who design our world.

1. Vicente Verdú, "Simulacro de Salvación," *A&V Monografías de Arquitectura y Vivienda 12: Casa, Cuerpo y Sueños* (1987):2.
2. Luís Fernández-Galiano, "El fuego del hogar: La producción histórica del espacio isotérmico," *A&V Monografías de Arquitectura y Vivienda 14: El espacio privado* (1987): 33.
3. Luís Fernández-Galiano, "Arquitectura, cuerpo, lenguaje: Páginas de un diccionario de fragmentos," *A&V Monofrafías de Arquitectura y Vivienda 12: Casa, Cuerpo y Sueños* (1987): 15.
4. Sir Banister Fletcher, *A History of Architecture* (London: Butterworths London, 1987 [19th edition] First edition: 1896).
5. Aldo Rossi, *A Scientific Autobiography,* (Cambridge: Oppositions books, The MIT Press, 1981).
6. Marc Antoine Laugier, *Essai sur l' architecture,* 1753.
7. Le Corbusier, *Vers une architecture,* Paris:1923.
8. Kenneth Frampton, *Modern Architecture: A Critical History,* (London: Thames and Hudson, Ltd., 1992 [Third edition]), 196.
9. Ibid.,196.
10. Philip Johnson, "House at New Canaan, Connecticut," *Architectural Record* (September 1950): 152.
11. *Capricho* translates literally as Caprice, a whim or a keen desire. Goya's personal series of etchings are often referred to as *Caprichos* because they were made at home, not commissioned.

Gae Aulenti

Milan, Italy 1976

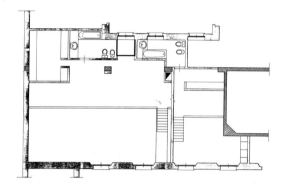

Italian architect Gae Aulenti's Milan apartment reunites many years of the architect's ideas, experiments, and domestic philosophies. Of all the houses included in this book, this is one of the spaces that best addresses the extended idea of home. The great detailing, which is useful—structural—rather than ornamental, reveals the lives and tastes of the inhabitants. In spite of Aulenti's use of monumental symbolism in some of her works, such as her own residence at Gubbio, the Milan apartment speaks of convenience and comfort, with the familiar touch of personal belongings. Based on the collections of art, books, various complementary styles of furniture and rugs in evidence, one can only conclude that Gae Aulenti's home is where her things are.

Divided into a main room and a studio space, Aulenti's apartment consists of two floors connected by a stairway and a small bridge which unify the space and improve circulation. The apartment was designed as a large container with just three closing doors—the main access, a bedroom door, and a kitchen door. The divisions between spaces are accomplished subtly with furniture, bookcases, changes in floor covering, and a deep closet space between the kitchen and dining room. Aulenti was very careful not to establish dependencies between objects and pieces of furniture, nor between these and the space, so that everything inside the container could be moved as needed. From the beginning, she aimed to design a place that would serve its inhabitants rather than requiring special care and specific usage.

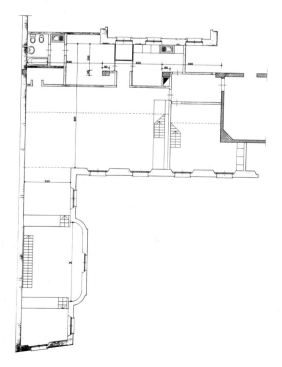

Considering Aulenti's approach to her home, it is easy to understand why she has become a favorite architect among museum directors and curators. In recent years she has renovated the huge Gare d'Orsay in Paris into France's major museum for nineteenth-century art. She has also recently completed a major renovation of the eighteenth-century Palazzo Grassi in Venice for new use as an art museum.

Opposite page: Plans.

Left & above: The living room and library include an eclectic combination of objects and furniture such as the Wassily chair (Breuer, 1925) in the foreground, the Parola standard lamp and Patrocla lamp, designed by Aulenti, and a hanging rug by Roy Lichtenstein.

19

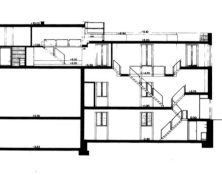

Above: Longitudinal section.

Right: Bathroom view. The bathroom, situated above the bedroom, is decorated with the same attention to detail. On the occasional table is the famous Pipistrello lamp, designed by Aulenti.

View of the bedroom, showing the spatial relationship
between the bedroom and the
bathroom at the upper left.

Above: The dining room, with lamps designed by Noguchi.

Below: Detail of the library with Aulenti's Ruspa lamp in the foreground.

Opposite: The terrace gallery.

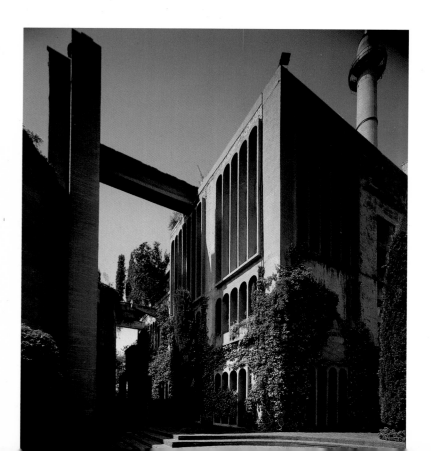

Ricardo Bofill

Barcelona, Spain 1973-75

The old cement factory where Ricardo Bofill's home in Barcelona is located was built around the end of the nineteenth century at a time when Barcelona was becoming an industrial city. A number of structures were eventually added to the original building as the size and needs of the factory changed.

The place is reminiscent of the opera set it resembled when Bofill first saw it. The Catalan architect was impressed by the immense silos and by a tall stack that marked the factory. Inside the building there were four kilometers of underground galleries that offered great possibilities for architectural intervention. The surreal proportions of the building's elements and its disjointed assembly now play an important role in the atmosphere of the home and studios. The studio, "Taller de Arquitectura," was installed first. By the end of the 1980s, after several additions and remodelings, the factory also became the architect's home. Bofill considers the building an example of the type of architecture his firm produces, such as the several postmodern subdivisions around Paris where he has designed large complexes of apartment buildings in a classical vocabulary.

Today, the factory maintains an impressive stage-like quality with subtly delimited areas of intervention. On the ground floor there is a very large room that Bofill calls "the Cathedral," which overlooks the enclosed patio. He uses the Cathedral for parties, as a conference hall, an exhibition space, or even as a garage. The so-called "Cubic Room" is where the architect's living room is located. Of unusual proportions, this space contains a working area as well as an intimate dining room whose table is always set in an intriguing manner, as if expecting something to happen. Objects lose scale and look toy-like in the face of the house's dimensions. There is an outdoor garden on a terrace adjacent to the dining room where the architect built a transparent sauna for bathing "outdoors." All over the house there are enigmatic doors that lead to unseen pathways. The ambiguous, contradictory elements of scale, shape, and juxtaposition define the surreal atmosphere of the factory-home of Ricardo Bofill.

Opposite: Exterior view of the architect's studio and the approach to the house.

Far left: Detail of the facade.

Left & below: Details of "the Cathedral." In the large picture, the enclosed courtyard is to the left, and above is a partial view through the windows of the cubic living room.

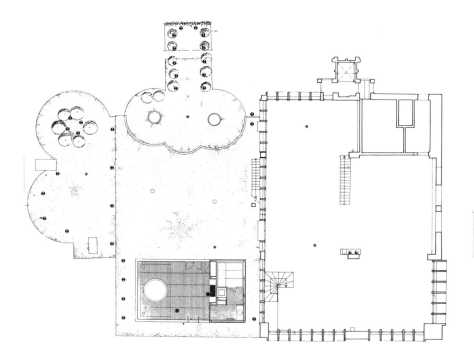

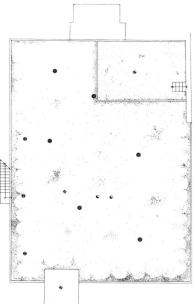

Right: Plan of the cubic living room and the sauna in the upper garden.

Below: View of the enclosed courtyard.

Left & top: Two views of the cubic living room.

Above: Detail of the dining room, with chairs by Mackintosh.

27

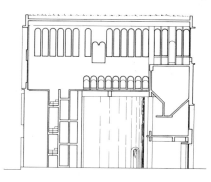

Top: Section showing the house's vertical circulation.

Above: View of the main kitchen.

Right: View of the pink room, in which the horizontal character of the furniture contrasts with the marked verticality of the space.

Exterior view of the transparent sauna in the upper garden.

Massimo & Gabriella Carmassi

Pisa, Italy 1992

The three-story office and home of the Italian architects Gabriella Ioli and Massimo Carmassi is a renovation of a residential structure originally built before the Renaissance, then enlarged at later dates. The present building maintains the brick and stone structure typical of Italian domestic architecture during the twelfth century. The main facade and the perimeter supporting walls contain elements that have remained untouched since a Renaissance addition was made, but the facade also reveals the continuous additions the building has undergone until the Carmassis' latest remodeling. As the Carmassis renovated, they tried to maintain the building's visible history without giving up the modern elements that make their lives comfortable. Their intervention is subtle, yet complete—rooms featuring delicate painted moldings are furnished in modern furniture that is sensitive to the history of its setting. The arch of the mezzanine above the library pays respect to the historic arch of the living room vault, yet is enclosed in glass framed in stainless steel—delicate materials that make a contemporary statement without interrupting the more massive volumes of the historic building. Likewise, the spiral stairway is a whispy structure enclosed in a thick tube that maintains the solidity of the surrounding walls, allowing the stairway to be light, practical, without contradicting the style of the building. This simultaneous sensitivity to restoration and innovation in architectural and interior design is characteristic of Massimo Carmassi's work on such projects as his restoration of the Teatro Verdi in Pisa.

Facades and elevations of the house, showing architectural elements from different periods.

Left & top: Details of the junction of the old building and the new architectural intervention, including the glassed-in private library.

Above: Section.

Right: Detail of the spiral stairs.

Above: An access doorway to the tubular stairwell.

Above: Section.

Left & below: Two views of the main living
room with furniture by Le Corbusier.

The bathroom allows direct access to the courtyard.

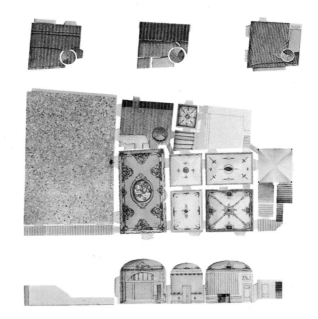

Above: Plans showing ceiling and wall decoration.

Below: Views of two rooms of the studio.

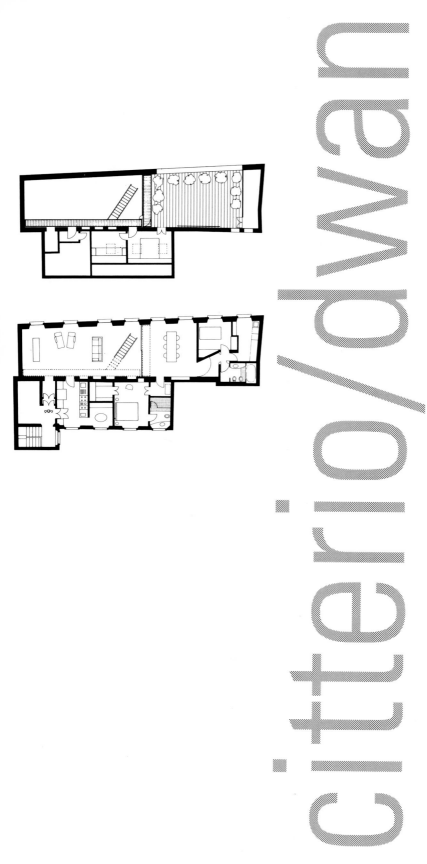

Antonio Citterio and Terry Dwan

Milan, Italy 1986–88

The Citterio/Dwan apartment is located in a seventeenth-century palazzo, which was subdivided and sold in pieces in the 1940s. The building was in a state of great disrepair when the Citterio studio began renovation in 1985. The most difficult aspect of the project was the decision to make a modern intervention in the seventeenth-century palazzo.

The apartment of architects Antonio Citterio and Terry Dwan is housed primarily in the original servants' quarters. The architects enlarged the mansard in order to extend the highest point of the ceiling to seventeen feet. The ceilings and floors of the apartment were completely rebuilt in order to acoustically and physically isolate the living quarters from the piano nobile below, which retains its coffered ceilings and original seventeenth-century decoration.

Immediately behind the dining area is a guest room with a private bath. A large door separates the guest apartment from the public areas of the house. The three bedroom/bath nuclei are completely isolated, including the one upstairs, which faces directly onto the terrace, with french doors into both bathroom and bedroom.

The idea of interconnecting interior and exterior was enforced in this project by further developing the sequence of the Italian palazzo block, which connects interiors and exteriors through a series of spaces, porticos, or semi-public courtyards. The architects added a terrace to the house by cutting away part of the roof facing the main thoroughfare of Via Brera. The glassed catwalk between terrace and house also acts as a skylight, while the library shelves inside provide a counterpoint to its lightness. The steel balcony inside the house rests on beams embedded in the wall, and is surfaced in perforated steel sheeting. Ochre-colored stucco was applied on the facade because of this material's historic use in Milan as an exterior treatment, and its contrast to the stainless steel finishes.

Opposite page: Upper and lower
floor plans.

Left: The interior courtyard of the
building containing the architects' apartment.

Above: The apartment's terrace.

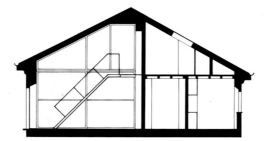

Right: Section.

Below: The passage to the terrace from the library.

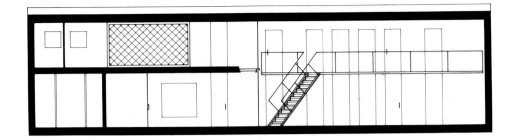

Left: Longitudinal section.

Below: A general view of the living room, dining room, and library toward the terrace.

Opposite page: View from the stairs of the living room, with furniture designed by Citterio himself and by Ettore Sottsass, among others. The painting is by Alexander Calder.

Below & left: Views of the dining room, kitchen, and breakfast nook.

David Chipperfield

London, England 1985

Chipperfield explains that designing his own apartment offered him opportunities often denied by clients, especially at the beginning of his architectural career. The conversion of a large ground floor and basement flat gave this British architect the chance to define an approach that was to become consistent in all his renovation projects.

The approach was a response to the limits of craft imposed by the on-site construction, as opposed to the control attainable in a workshop. By dividing the construction process into areas related to the shell of the building, and the elements inside it, he achieved a dynamic process normally not available on site or on the drawing board. With a planning strategy that differentiated between crafts to be developed, and maintenance of construction rhythm, the locations of elements within the building were decided and on-site construction began, while craft elements were still being developed through discussion in the workshop. This process of building and designing at the same time is called fast-tracking.

By organizing the construction procedure in this way, Chipperfield aimed to best use the character, fabric, and organization of the existing building. The layout of spaces follows the original internal divisions on the ground floor, with bedrooms and bathrooms on the basement floor, connected by a staircase and a light-well. A clay-tiled vaulted ceiling determines the planning of the basement floor.

Through the use of interior windows, the house has an airy quality which is heightened by the modern furniture and open railings. The interior views framed by these openings join the spaces visually, lending a sense of mobility and ease. The use of sleek, modern materials, such as the stainless steel, granite, and sycamore in the kitchen establishes a disparity between the elements introduced in the interior renovation and the Victorian detailing of the previously existing moldings and traditional London exterior. The styling of these materials also indicates the aesthetic that has attracted many Japanese clients to Chipperfield, who has built a number of projects in Japan.

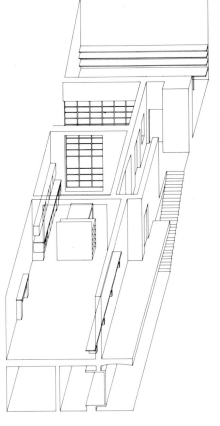

Opposite page: View of the facade.

Left: View of the corridor leading to the stairs with the original stone vault, which the architect opted to conserve.

Above: Axonometric drawing of the apartment.

The living and dining room, furnished with armchairs by Le Corbusier and a divan by Eileen Gray.

Left: View from the dining room toward the kitchen.

Above: The view across the dining space. The Spartana chairs are by Hans Coray (1938).

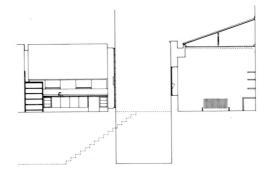

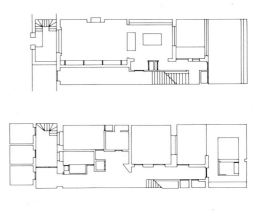

Opposite page: View through the stairs leading up to the architect's studio.

Top: Section and plans of the upper and lower floors.

Above: View of the architect's studio on the upper floor of the house.

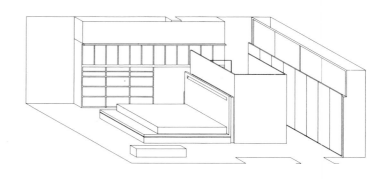

Above: Detail of the stairs and the handrail.

Above right: Axonometric drawing of the master bedroom.

Right: View through the interior window of the children's bedroom.

The master bedroom with the bathroom beyond.

Aurelio Galfetti

Bellinzona (Ticino), Switzerland 1987

Aurelio Galfetti is one of a number of internationally known architects who works primarily in southern Switzerland and northern Italy. Galfetti has completed numerous projects in Bellinzona, which is characterized by the thirty-three-hundred-foot mountains flanking the valley in which it is located, and the two walls that hem the city. While Galfetti does not believe in appropriating, and decontextualizing, the history of the region in his projects, he does base many of his architectural ideas on a conceptual, collective memory of Bellinzona history. This approach shows in the parallel walls of Galfetti's community tennis center, and the dialogue between old and new in his restoration of the Castelgrande, the oldest of three castles in Bellinzona.

Galfetti's home is in one of two compact reinforced concrete structures, one of which is black (Casa Nera), and the other, white (Casa Bianca). The buildings are perfectly symmetrical cubes, each four floors high. The exterior treatment of Casa Bianca and Casa Nera (as well as the Villa on Via Mirasole in Bellinzona,1985) shows Galfetti's interest in layering and differentiated facade treatments. On Casa Bianca and Casa Nera, the joints of the construction forms are articulated by the insertion of granite strips during pouring, so that they become part of the wall, offsetting the interior planes which are carved out of the volume and finished in white. Galfetti located his home in Casa Nera, occupying the top three floors.

The rational, symmetrical interior layout of the apartment has been seen in some of Galfetti's previous projects, such as the Villa on Via Mirasole. Galfetti's top-floor apartments often have gardens or pools on the roof, just as in his own residence, which includes a rooftop garden, pool, and solarium. The void between the roof and the top-floor walls allows natural light to flood the upper-story spaces, especially the terrace. Inside the house, adjacent to the terrace, are the kitchen, living room, library, and the main bedroom. One floor below are the children's rooms and bathrooms, as well as a separate kitchenette which allows them a certain independence. Many of the interior finishes, such as the kitchen island and the terrace paving, echo the facade articulation. All interior effects are black and white.

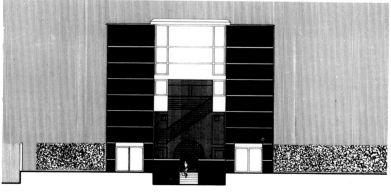

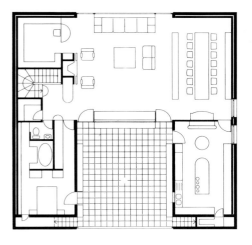

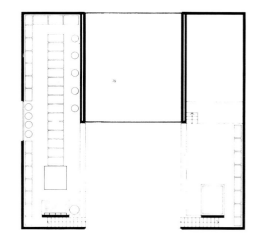

Opposite top: View of the building standing in the middle of the valley with one of the three castles of Bellinzona on the hill.

Opposite Bottom: A rendering showing details of the entryway.

Top: Plans of the main floor and the upper terrace.

Above: Views of the double-height living room and its courtyard.

Following page: The dining room with a view across the living room and into the library. The chairs are by Gio Ponti (Superleggera, 1957).

Previous page: The living room with the library in the background. The armchairs and soft chairs were designed by Le Corbusier, and the sofa was designed by Galfetti himself.

This page, clockwise: Views of the kitchen, the library, the main bedroom seen from the courtyard, and the interior courtyard. All the interior decoration is black and white.

Opposite page: Stairs lead to the upper terrace and garden.

gehry

Frank O. Gehry

Santa Monica, California 1978–94

In less than fifteen years, Frank Gehry has remodeled his Santa Monica home twice. The Canadian-born architect first remodeled in 1978 based on a detailed study he had made on the construction possibilities of the recently acquired building. The suburban characteristics of the neighborhood in which the house is located and the growing and changing needs of Gehry's family were taken into account in his intervention in the building.

Gehry enjoyed the iconic quality of the house and decided to keep its original structure. Around it, he organized a series of interconnected volumes that were to answer the family's needs. He located the living, dining, and kitchen areas, and his son's room on the ground floor. On the second floor, he demolished partitions to enlarge the master bedroom and bathroom, and created another child's room for the future. In the first remodeling Gehry used materials normally used in industrial architecture; during the second intervention, however, he used more refined materials. One continuous feature of the house is its many interior windows, skylights, and various openings including those of chain-link fence and wire-reinforced glass. These openings of all kinds constantly reveal, reflect, refract, and frame different views and elements of the house and surrounding grounds.

Gehry never intended his home to be a static form, and due to the family's changing needs he decided to remodel it again in 1992. He intended his house to grow, to change while its inhabitants were doing so.

The new floor plan is similar to the old one. The hall, kitchen, and dining room have remained in a narrow U-shaped space on the ground floor of the house. On the upper floor, Gehry's son's old bedroom has been turned into a studio, and part of his own bedroom floor has been replaced by a glass piece that allows natural light to reach the ground floor. Outdoors, apple-green ceramic tiles have been laid around a new pool, while the old garage, previously used as a guest room, has been turned into a children's play area. The house represents one source of the design sensibilities Gehry has incorporated into such projects as the new American Center in Paris and the forthcoming Disney concert hall in Los Angeles.

Opposite top: The main door.

Opposite below: A door leading from the garden into the dining room.

Below: The principal facade.

Opposite page: The side facade.

Above: The gallery added on to the architect's bedroom in the latest remodeling.

Right: A view of the new bedroom with the gallery in the background. The seating was designed by Gehry.

The dining room with direct access to the kitchen and the garden.
The chairs were designed by Gehry for Knoll.

The rear facade and swimming pool. A large sliding door opens onto the patio.

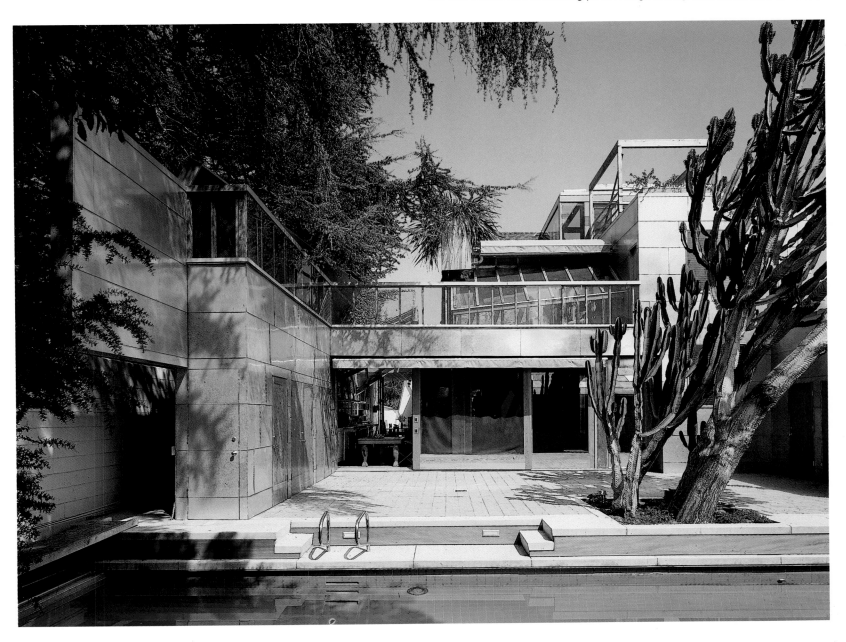

The former guest room is now a playroom for Gehry's children.

The playroom.

Michael Graves

Princeton, New Jersey 1987–92

For his home, American architect Michael Graves remodeled a warehouse originally built in 1926. The well-proportioned building was designed in a classically Tuscan vernacular style by Italian stonemasons who were employed at the time in construction at Princeton University, where Graves has taught for over twenty years.

The warehouse has an L-shaped floor plan, and is built of hollow clay tile, brick, and stucco. Graves maintained the facade's structural simplicity, but added postmodern classical elements that refer to the building's ultimate sources. The first section Graves rehabilitated, the north wing of the building, contains the ground-floor living area, dining room, library, and a garden terrace. The master bedroom and Graves's studio are on the upper floor. Both floors can be accessed from the exterior patio, which was incorporated into the old building's service alley. In 1992, Graves renovated the west wing, where he built several multi-use rooms as well as additional bedrooms. Formal gardens flank the house, which is at the end of a long drive where an arbor covered in wisteria opens onto a spacious lawn.

The interior finishes and the furnishings are largely neoclassical and echo the influences referred to on the facade. The soft colors and the range of references exemplify the postmodern style of architecture, here quite restrained, for which Graves is known in projects such as his hotels for Disney theme parks, the Portland Building (Portland, Oregon, 1980), and in his well-known designs for furniture, rugs, and other objects.

Above: The facade of the house.

Right: The entrance.

Opposite page: The entrance rotunda, with doorways leading into the rooms of the house. Natural light filters in from above.

Above left: The glass roof of the library lets in daylight and opens up the narrow space.

Above right: A work area.

Michael Graves is one of the leading figures of postmodernism. His home reveals an eclectic combination of different architectural references, as seen here in the dining room and bathroom, and on the previous page in the study.

Hiroshi Hara

Machida, Japan 1973–74

The house of Japanese architect Hiroshi Hara and his architect wife, Wakana Kitagawa, is located at the base of a hill near Tokyo, surrounded by dense woods which belong to their neighbor. The Haras therefore enjoy the Japanese notion of shakkei, "borrowing landscape" by incorporating it into their house. Nature surrounds the house, and therefore the architecture is produced as part of nature. Hara's home, in its woodland valley location, illustrates several principles that he has announced in a series of manifestos defining the microcosm inside the home, including "Architecture as a valley" and "The city inside the house." Many of Hara's houses are built metaphors for urban design, complete with spaces that resemble plazas, streets, intersections, and landmarks. The multi-layered architecture created by the boundaries of the building, the cloudlike frosted skylights inside, and the system of paths between the volumes of the rooms, is seem in other Hara projects, such as Yamamoto International in Tokyo (1987) and the Tasaki Museum in Karuizawa (1986).

Hara's house has a double roof made of translucent and transparent prefabricated panels supported by a metal framework. By means of a series of curved interior windows, the light that enters this double roof is distributed throughout the house. At night, the removal of the translucent roof allows a magnificent view of the starry sky in the middle of the woods.

The house is twenty years old, and since it was built it has hardly been changed. Hara compares his home to the Buddhist literature he admires, in which two main concepts are defined: nothingness and glorification. The death of Hara's father during the design process made him choose to glorify the building, and since then Hara has applied the same idea of glorification of space in many of his architectural projects.

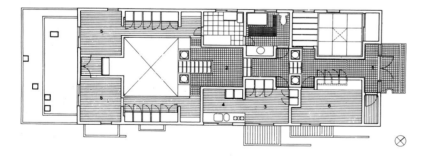

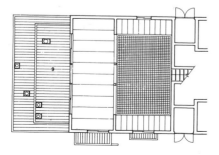

Opposite top: The Hara house in the midst of the woods follows the Japanese *shakkei* school of landscaping.

Opposite bottom: Plans of the upper and lower floors.

Left: Passageway to the courtyard.

Below: Inside view toward the entrance.

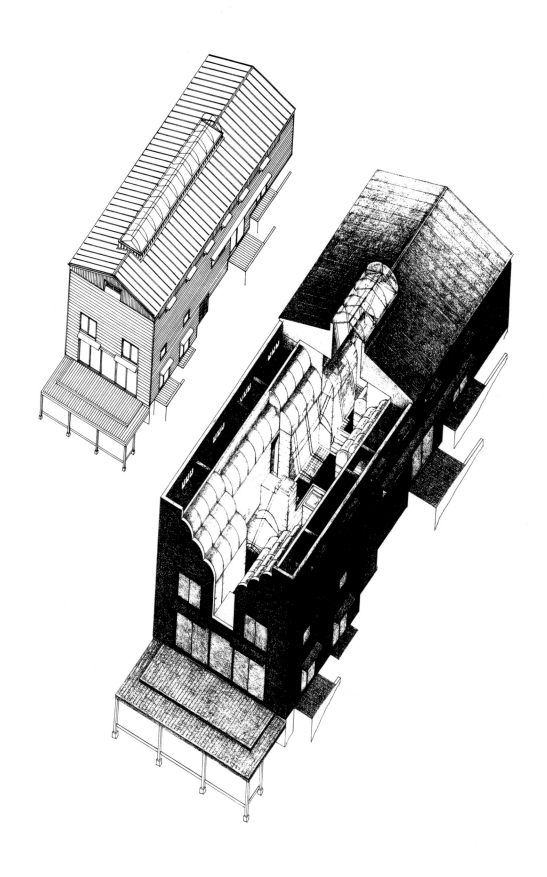

Opposite page: Axonometric view of the house, and cutaway showing the interior skylight system and main hallway.

Right: The entrance facade.

Far right: View through the entrance.

Below: View of the living room.

Norihide Imagawa

imagawa

Tokyo, Japan 1987

Norihide Imagawa's "Mint House" seems almost as if it was designed inside-out. The rooms look inward for their light, and windows face onto the central stairway. At one point, these stairs seem to become a central courtyard, with various houses facing onto it. Like a courtyard, this stairwell atrium provides a central core of light to Imagawa's house. The atrium and the rooms around it are encased in a glazed framework which protects the interior from the elements. Most of the non-concrete sections of the house were prefabricated as part of a unique construction system devised by Imagawa.

A half-story down from the entry is the living room, a semi-subterranean room that receives light through full-wall sliding doors. These doors open onto a narrow patio sheltered by a concrete wall and planting boxes on street-level. On the main floor are the master bedroom, dining room, kitchen, and den, with two bedrooms, a large balcony, and a guest room on the top level. Many of the fascinating details of the house are in the structure—the steel reinforcing rods that criss-cross the wide windows, the expanded metal lath of the entryway ceiling, the joining of metal to wood, and wood to concrete, and the irregular spotted grid of the reinforced concrete. The combination of industrial materials and a new construction technique with warm wood finishes is a successful marriage of technology and a traditional Japanese aesthetic.

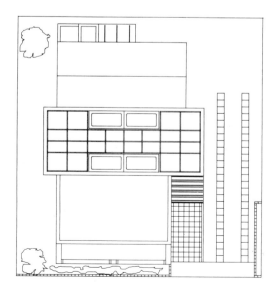

Opposite page: Exterior view of the house; site plan.

Left: Detail of the canopy.

Top: Side facade.

Above: Access door.

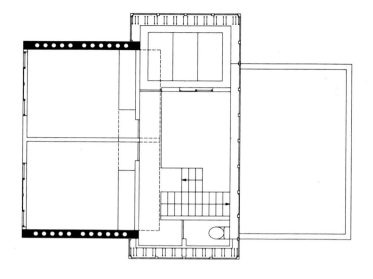

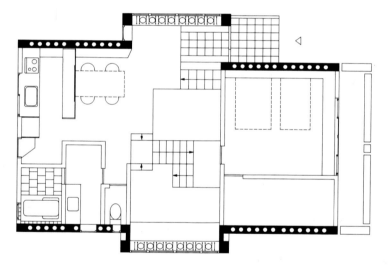

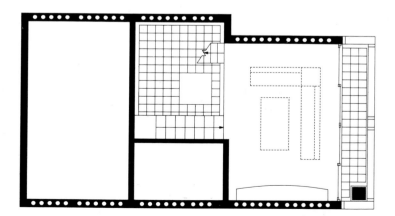

Right: Floor plans.

Opposite: Facades of the house in daylight and after dark, showing the variety of building materials.

Above: View from the entryway into the dining room.

Middle & right: In the various transitional zones, the junctions of metal and concrete with wood are evidence of fine craftsmanship.

Below right: Study area.

Below left: The children's area on the upper floor.

Bottom: Two views of the living room.

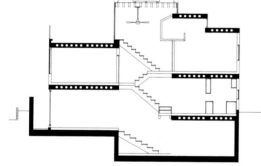

Above: Longitudinal section.

Right: Detail of the stairs seen from the dining room.

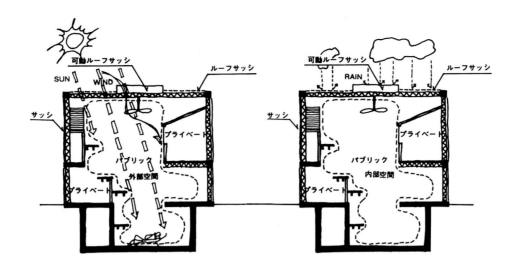

Above: Climatological study for the house.

Below: The interior courtyard viewed from the top of the stairs.

Arata Isozaki

Karuizawa, Japan 1984–88

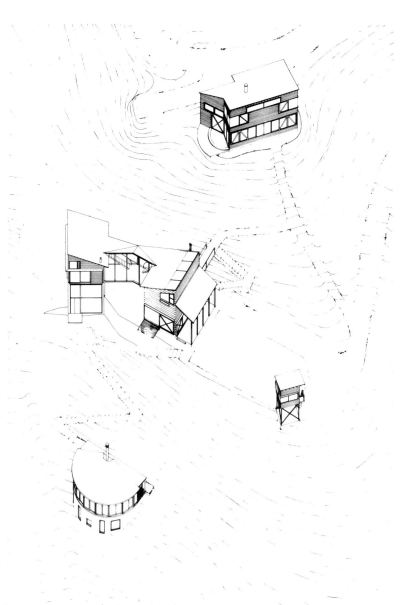

On a steep slope in a wooded valley in Karuizawa, Arata Isozaki, his sculptor wife, Aiko Miyawaki, the writer Kunio Tsuji, and his wife, Sahoko, have a summer residence consisting of a series of four buildings. Known in America for his designs for the Museum of Contemporary Art in Los Angeles and a major expansion program for the Brooklyn Museum in New York, Isozaki designed his personal housing complex so that each of the residents could enjoy a private studio. Budget and site restrictions made it necessary to use simple volumes, and the buildings are constructed of wood, which is painted black, allowing the buildings to blend into the forest setting. This same finish was used for Isozaki's Hara Museum ARC in Gunma, Japan (1987–88), indicating the pastoral nature of the project, as opposed to his urban constructions.

The Tsuji couple's house sits at the top of the site, and was built in the mid-seventies. On the middle level of the site is Miyawaki's atelier, with a small bedroom and kitchen on the ground floor. A separate study called the "treehouse" faces toward Mt. Asama, and contains a Murphy bed and writing area for Isozaki. Between the atelier and study is a moss garden, which holds a preliminary version of Miyawaki's sculptural work *Utsurohi*. Isozaki originally intended to include living quarters for himself on the middle part of the site, but ultimately this plan was abandoned. Down the hill from the atelier and study is a semicircular pavilion that includes the couple's living room, dining room, and kitchen facing the curved, glass facade that offers a one-hundred-eighty-degree view. On the lower floor are two guest bedrooms, a bathroom, and a sauna.

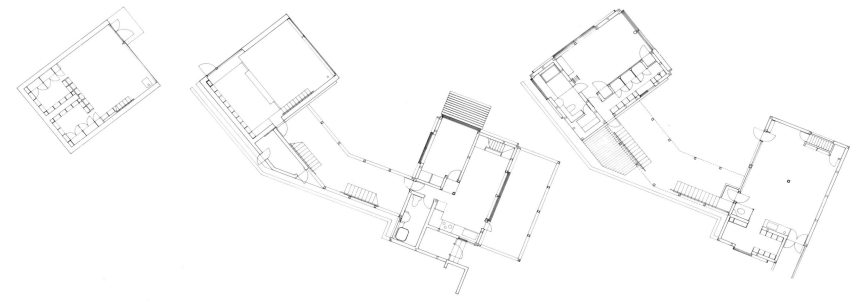

Opposite page: Site plan.

Top: Plan of the atelier.

Above & left: Views of the atelier and the "treehouse" studio with Aiko Miyawaki's sculpture, *Utsuroi,* in the foreground.

Opposite page: Detail of the atelier, which offers fragmentary views of the surrounding woods.

Above & left: View of the interior and the porch of Miyawaki's studio, with details of her sculptures.

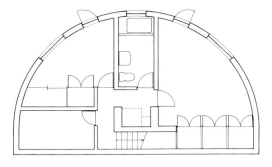

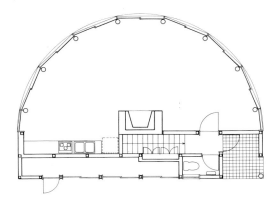

Opposite page: The semicircular pavilion.

Top: Plans of the pavilion.

Above: View of the interior. The dining chairs were designed by Isozaki himself, while the armchair in the background is by Eames.

Toyo Ito

Tokyo, Japan 1984

Toyo Ito sought a difficult balance between primitivism (understood as simplicity) and modernity when he designed his home in Tokyo. The juxtaposition of traditional Japanese residential concepts, both traditional and modern industrial building materials, and ultramodern furnishings, makes his "Silver Hut" a fascinating study of the contrasting—and simultaneously mutually supportive—concepts of primitivism and technology.

Ito's home is roofed by seven vaults organized around a covered central patio. Six small vaults cover the living and dining rooms, kitchen, bedrooms, and Japanese room, while the largest, central vault over the courtyard includes a manually-operated tent canvas that can be retracted to open the space to the sky.

Except for the area where the family bedrooms are located, Ito's home is only one story high, but it is perceived as a single volume since part of the bedroom area is underground. The house combines aluminum and zinc alloy panels with Japanese building materials such as tatami floor mats, and ceramic floor tiles typical of Japanese folk houses. The seven vaults are supported on concrete pillars spaced on a grid, so that the wall panels do not support any structural load, and can be moved open or shut just as in traditional Japanese house plans. Most of the furniture is made of industrial metals and can be adjusted to different heights according to the user's needs. The vaults covering the rooms are lightweight, prefabricated structures framed in aluminum, and perforated by twenty-three lightwells which, besides allowing an intense natural light, give the house's occupants the sense of being in an airplane. The contradictory senses of traditionalism and space-age technology present a gentle paradox in Ito's Silver Hut.

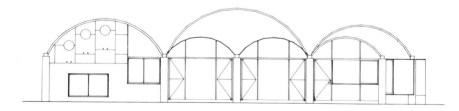

Top: Aerial view of the house.

Above: Elevation.

Opposite page: Plan; views of the enclosed courtyard with the folding roof.

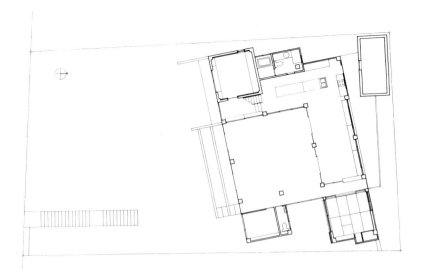

The kitchen, which
recieves natural light
from overhead portholes.

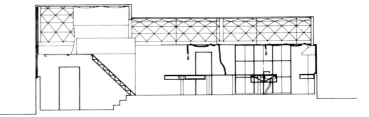

Left: Detail of the kitchen.

Above: Section plan of the kitchen.

Carlos Jiménez

Houston, Texas 1983–1994

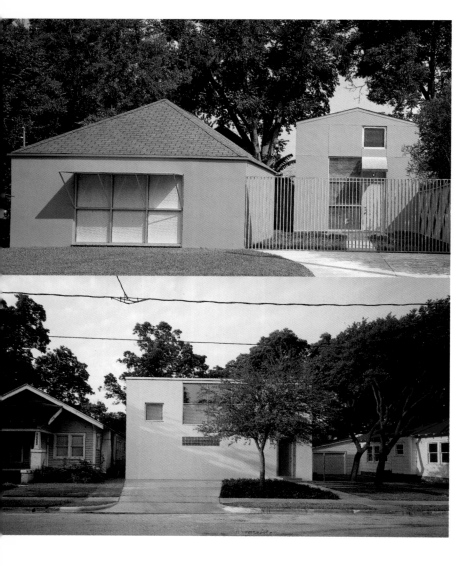

Located near downtown Houston, this house and studio complex reflects an incremental architectural progression of an eleven-year period and marks the evolution implicit in such processes. The original house was Jiménez's first built architectural work—a practical demonstration of his ideas. The forms and volumes used then have remained essentially the same throughout the various transformations. Spatial elements have been added or removed at each renovation, yet these exploratory actions have reinforced the simplicity of the structure. Jiménez's house and studio complex has proven to be an architecture that, because of its simplicity, allows for subtle variations and transformations.

The first group of structures, built in 1983–84, consisted of a one-story studio/living unit, a separate two-story library tower in the rear, and an eight-foot-high wooden frame enclosing a courtyard and garden. In 1986, a two-story building was built parallel to the initial construction, but set back in the property. In 1990 Jiménez linked it with the adjacent library tower. All these structures were built of concrete block, finished with a smooth stucco, and painted a unifying blue. This neutral color provides an ever-changing interplay of light and shadow throughout the seasons. The abundance of natural light in each building dissolves the compactness of the geometry. The aluminum windows, granite sills, steel door frames, structural glass, and multicolored transparencies provide varying textures on the intense blue walls.

The newest addition to the compound, the house finished in 1994, runs perpendicular to the first three buildings across the street. Built of the same materials as the previous structures, the stucco finish in this case is painted a neutral gray, echoing the stucco's natural grayish patina. The scale of this building makes direct references to its predecessors, but inside it is more compartmentalized. The two-story house consists of a large open living, dining, and kitchen area on the upper level, and two bedrooms with their corresponding bathrooms on the ground floor.

Top & left: Exterior views of the studio and the house.

Opposite page: Plan of the complex and (top to bottom) Jiménez's studio; looking toward the house; view of the house.

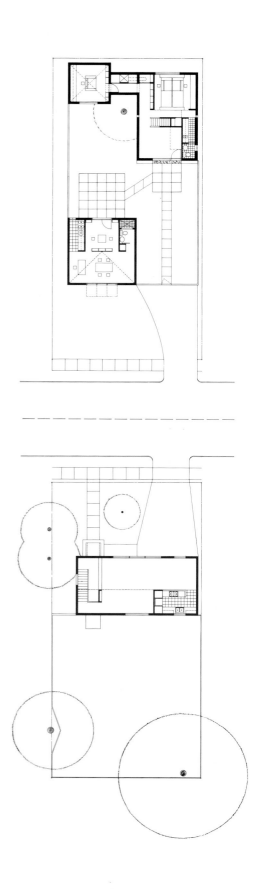

1983   1986   1990

Page 92, top: Evolution of the plans for the complex.

Page 92, bottom: Interiors of the studio.

Page 93: Detail of the interplay of shapes and volumes in the studio.

Above: Kitchen and living area of the original house.

Opposite top: Plans and elevations of the new house across the street from the studio complex.

Opposite bottom: View of the living area, with seating from Mies van der Rohe's Barcelona collection and the black Varius chair designed by Oscar Tusquets.

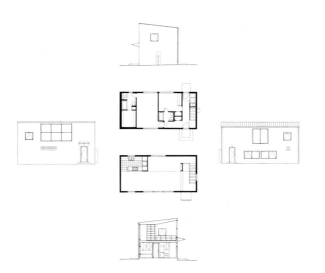

jourda
perraudin

Jourda & Perraudin

Lyon, France 1987

These architects of the technologically advanced Parilly Metro Station in Lyon gradually formulated the interior layout of their home based on their evolving needs with their four growing children, with conceptual references to Le Corbusier's Heidi Weber Pavilion in Zurich.

The property is in Lyon, surrounded by a high fence. In order to maintain most of the vegetation, the architects restricted the foundation of the house to a few specific points. This resulted in a house that is more a floating pavilion than a conventional structure.

A prefabricated metal support structure allowed for rapid construction and the house was assembled in just a few days. It simply consists of a number of identical block-shaped units arranged in a line. A canopy raised on a framework over the main structure is intended to look like an extension of the neighboring trees. This concept was used earlier in Jourda and Perraudin's School of Architecture, also in Lyon (1982).

The interior is finished in the plywood commonly used in Europe for fruit and vegetable containers found in open-air markets. This rustic finish contrasts with the vaulted ceilings over the main living space, which imply a grand, formal interior.

The north and west facades of Jourda and Perraudin's home were left almost completely solid, while the main facade to the south is transparent. This open wall allows the indoor space to flow into the garden surrounding the house. Terraces sheltered by the house's canopy emphasize this relationship and soften the boundaries between indoor and outdoor activities.

Top: The principal facade.

Bottom: The doorway onto the patio.

Opposite top: Elevation of the structure showing the relationship between the house's interior and exterior spaces.

Opposite bottom: Exterior view of the main patio and living area.

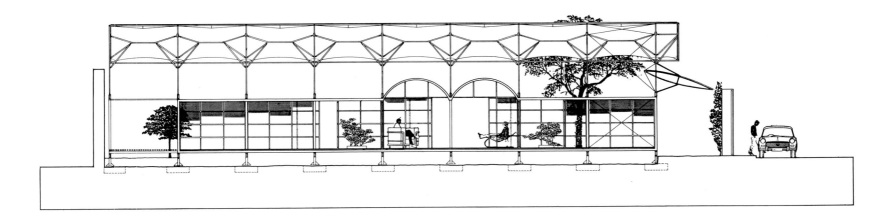

Below: Living and dining room with the library in the background, separated by a transparent partition. The dining table was designed by Le Corbusier.

Below right: Detail of interior and exterior glass walls.

Opposite page: View of the living room toward the garden. The sofa and chaise longue were also designed by Le Corbusier.

Ricardo Legorreta

Valle de Bravo, Mexico 1974

The Legorretas were primarily concerned with two issues regarding their weekend home—they wanted it to be well integrated into its hillside forest setting, and also to be a flexible and comfortable informal place. Ricardo Legorreta is a Mexican architect who has achieved international recognition for his regionalist architectural style—his dedication to preserving Mexican tastes and traditional habits in his country's architecture. He also freely acknowledges his aesthetic debt to the great Mexican master Luis Barragán. These references can be identified in his house.

In his house design, Legorreta reinterpreted the architectural heritage and tradition of the area from his functionalist and contemporary perspective. The pitched roof of the house, according to the local architectural language, also mimicks the hill slope, achieving an integration between construction and landscape. From a distance the house appears to be submerged in the rich surrounding vegetation.

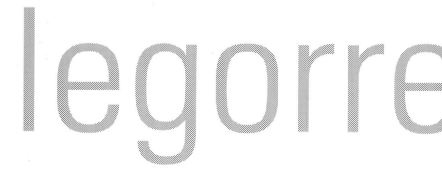

The outside of the house is painted in natural colors, and there is no formal planting, allowing the natural vegetation to surround, and even cover the house. The windows are placed based on their effect inside the house for the lighting and viewing needs of the rooms. The facade observes the simple language of local vernacular architecture, which is based not on the column and void of the International style of design, but the traditional Mexican emphasis of the solid wall, the enclosure, promoting privacy and reflection.

The main elements in the house—the master bedroom, the living area, and the children's room—are placed on three different platforms. Keeping furniture to a minimum ensures flexibility—rooms are available to be used as needed. The rustic style furnishings and neutral, earth tones prevailing throughout the house impart a sense of the traditional existence and Mexican architectural values that Legorreta espouses.

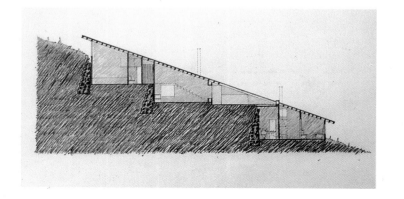

Opposite page, top: View of the exterior showing how the house adapts to the landscape.

Opposite page, bottom: Section.

Right: General plan.

Below, clockwise: Terrace view; living room; master bedroom; multi-purpose space.

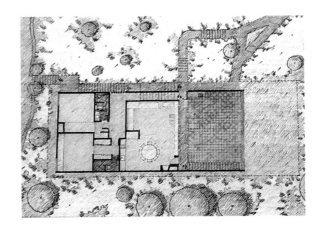

Georges Maurios

Paris, France 1990

Behind the buildings on the busy rue St. Jacques in Paris, there is a green area with public gardens, trees, and single family homes. One of these homes, a nineteenth-century villa, was enlarged and remodeled by French architect Georges Maurios as his home and studio. The studio is located in the original building, while Maurios's home is in the two-story addition he designed on top.

Maurios made the addition to the building as light as possible—less than thirty tons—so the old walls of the villa below could support it. The exterior walkway and stairs are designed not to add weight to the load.

Maurios likens his home to a suit cut by a good tailor. The home is adapted to the movements, gestures, and needs that make his everyday life comfortable. The interior is organized according to simple geometric principles—there are no strange corners, nor is there any extraneous ornament. Around a central core where the chimney is located, Maurios placed the living area, dining room, and kitchen. The upper section of a two-story wall is used for the library, which is accessible by means of a sliding glass walkway from the study upstairs. Several window openings provide selected views towards the neighboring gardens and the center of Paris. Maurios used natural wood and metal carpentry in an effort to do away with what he considers unnecessary trends. He followed lessons learned years ago from his teachers: Le Corbusier, with whom he worked in the development of Chandigarh, and Josep Lluís Sert, who was Dean of Harvard's Graduate School of Design when Maurios was a student there.

maurios

Opposite top: Elevation.

Opposite bottom, left & right: Views of the side and front facades showing the addition designed by the architect and its relationship with the original building.

Below left: Third floor exterior access corridor.

Below: Second-level courtyard with skylights giving light to the room below.

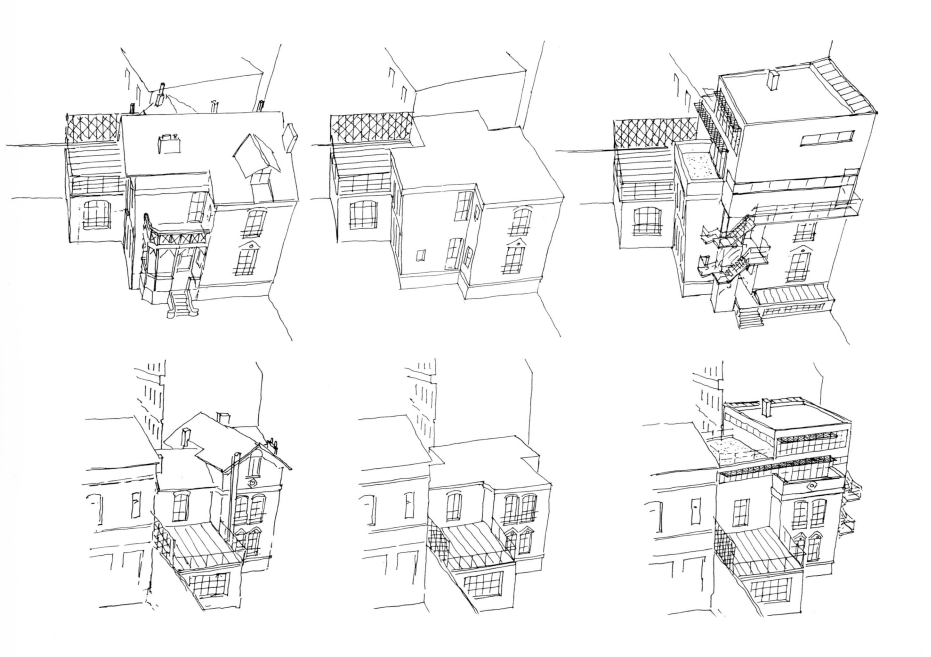

104

Opposite page: Evolution of the design of the extension.

Below: Four views of the living area around the central nucleus of the fire-place. The beige carpet and oval, chrome table were designed by Eileen Gray, and the cowhide chairs are by Le Corbusier. The bottom left picture shows the third-floor terrace and the double-height space with the library at the top.

The bathroom and main bedroom.

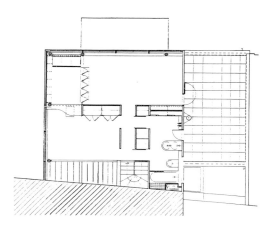

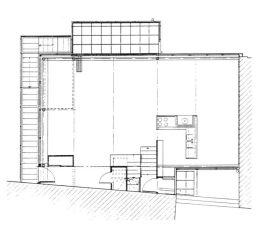

Top & bottom: Fourth- and third-floor plans.

Above: Two views of the fourth-floor studio with the sliding walkway to the library.

107

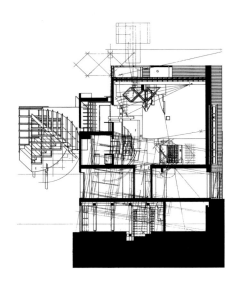

Thom Mayne (Morphosis)

Ocean Park, California 1988 (under construction)

Thom Mayne's Sixth Street House addresses the differences and tensions between objects and buildings. Ten steel units, including stairs, showers, skylights, and other utilitarian elements were built of found parts of machinery and incorporated into the redesign of the house. As objects which have lost their purpose, they provide an archaeology of contemporary culture, while at the same time, they embrace a new function in their recycled states.

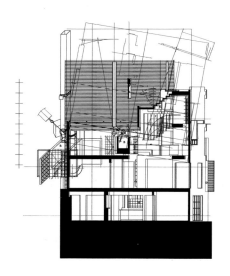

While the formal facade of Mayne's house is contextual and traditional, providing the outside world with a model of behavior toward the house's inhabitants, the discarded machinery, or dead tech, parts on the inside involve the inhabitants in a dialogue with the outside world. In this way, the architecture attempts to address conflicting demands for privacy and connection to society.

Thom Mayne, who is a principal of the California architectural firm Morphosis, transformed a duplex apartment into a two-bedroom house, which occupies the two upper levels, and a one-bedroom apartment located partially below ground-level. The foundation, perimeter walls, and floors of the duplex were reused, with the new wood-frame and cement composition board structure left uncovered. The twenty-four-foot-high main living space is meant to resemble the loft in which Mayne previously lived. Bedrooms are placed on the lower level, while the loft space accommodates a living/dining area, a kitchen, and a studio.

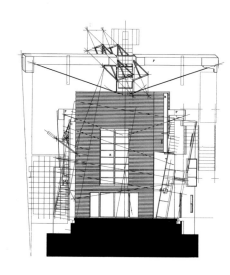

Mayne's house is a work in progress. The structure is a laboratory through which Mayne works out his architectural ideas at the same time as he inhabits the house. Built projects in which some of these ideas appear include Crawford House in Montecito, California (1990) and the Salick Healthcare Office Building in Los Angeles (1991).

mayne

Opposite page, top to bottom: Two sections; front elevation.

Below: Models showing the two sides of the house.

Right & bottom: Plans of the floors ranging from below-grade (bottom left) to roof plan (upper right). Showers and other details are shown in axonometric drawings.

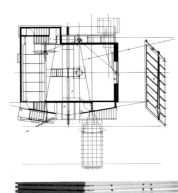

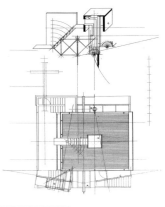

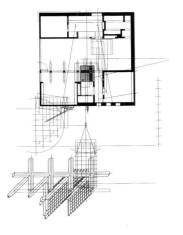

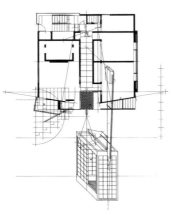

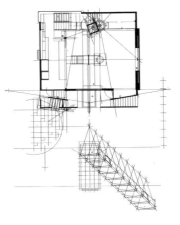

MECANOO (Francine Houven and Erick van Egeraat)

Rotterdam, Netherlands 1989–91

The site where the Dutch architects Francine Houben and Erick van Egeraat built their own studio and residence is located on the southern edge of the Kralingse Plas, a small lake on the outskirts of Rotterdam. Their house shares company with other houses, apartment blocks, and boat-houses designed by some of the Netherlands' most famous modern architects. The house is located at the end of a row of nineteenth-century buildings, and situated on a north-south axis, with the north side facing the lake and the south side facing a small canal.

The building is both a home and a working area for the van Egeraat-Houben family. A garage and a studio take up the ground floor. The living room is situated on the floor above because of the beautiful canal view. The kitchen and dining areas, located on the same floor, flow onto a spacious south-facing balcony which looks over the cozy inner court of gardens and the canal. The three bedrooms and the study/library are on the top floor, which is a double-height space rising from the dining area up to the study. The rooms are closely linked through horizontal and vertical connections—extra doors, unexpected pathways, spy-holes, and a pedestrian bridge form circuits that allow for formal and informal routes through the house.

Privacy and solar benefits were decisive factors in designing the house facade. The street side is fully glazed except for a thin column of concrete rising from the ground up to the flat roof. On the east side, the only exposed side wall is half-glazed, and protected from the sun and intrusion by a movable bamboo screen set in a metal frame. The rear, south-facing facade is constructed of wood panels, composite blocks, and glazing, and supports balconies with sunshades. On the ground floor, the concrete floor slab extends beyond the foundation to form the garden terrace. The choices and detailing of materials, colors, textures, and patterns for floors, walls, and ceilings were kept simple and refined.

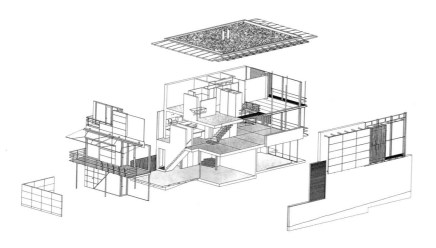

Opposite page, top: Rear facade with views of the canal.

Opposite, bottom: Axonometric sketch.

Left: The streetside facade.
Top: The house lit up at night.

Above: Detail of the rear balcony facing the courtyard.

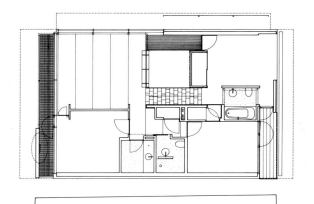

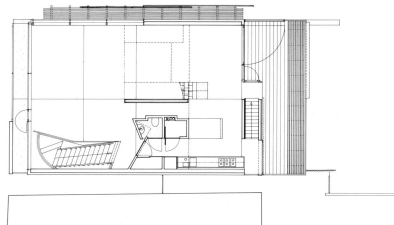

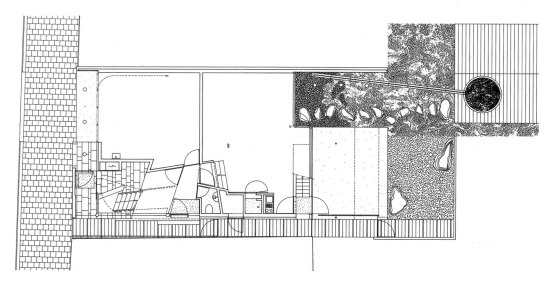

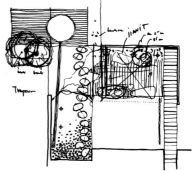

Opposite page, from top: Plans of the third, second, and ground floors.

Top, right: Looking into the architects' studio from the courtyard.

Left: A bamboo screen filters the sun.

Above: Garden plan.

Above: The double-height living and dining area.

Right: The stairway at the front of the house.

Opposite top: The library with views of the lake.

Opposite bottom: The stairway down from the library.

The ground-floor kitchen.

The dining room seen from the living room. The table was designed by architect Norman Foster and the chairs are by Herman Miller.

meier

Richard Meier

New York, New York 1972

Even though Richard Meier has lived in his apartment on the Upper East Side of Manhattan in New York for over twenty years, its pristine, classically modern design is as fresh today as when he first renovated the large duplex. The interiors are all white, as is traditional in Meier's residential work, and accented with built-in furniture of his own design, and other pieces designed in the 1920s by such renowned masters as Mies van der Rohe, whose Grand Confort chairs are in the living room, and Le Corbusier, whose M R armchairs are used at the dining room table.

In this apartment, the architect confined his major renovations to the lower floor, where he transformed a series of small, conventional rooms typical of New York apartments, into a large, open, and flowing space including the living room, dining room, library and study, entry area, and the kitchen to the rear. The entry, where a sweeping and elegant staircase ascends to the private quarters on the second level, is partially enclosed by a wall extending perpendicular from the side wall into the main space. On the other side of this interior wall, Meier has designed an ensemble of bookcase, couch, and desk that gives definition to the large space and integrates the living area. On the main floor, all of the old architectural details have been removed to enhance the light and the open loft-like space that is accented only by the furnishings, a large painting by Meier's long-time friend Frank Stella, and Meier's own collages.

On the upper floor, the long hallway and the adjacent bedrooms and bathrooms have been left essentially as they were originally built, but painted white to enhance the architectural detailing, which was left intact, and to unify the private quarters of the apartment.

Above: Stairs leading to the private quarters.

Opposite: The hall with a partial view of the library.

Above: The dining room with chairs by Mies van der Rohe and a painting by Franz Kline in the background.

Opposite page: Two views showing the relationship between the library, living room, and the dining room in the background. The armchairs in the living room are by Le Corbusier, and the painting is by Frank Stella. Note the built-in seating unit.

miralles

Enric Miralles and Benedetta Tagliabue

Barcelona, Spain 1993–94

The home of this Spanish and Italian team is in the old town of Barcelona, just outside the Gothic walls, in a building whose past is as rich and complex as it is difficult to define. When Miralles and Tagliabue first saw the building it was in a desperate state of disrepair. They decided to remodel the main apartment in the building, which featured an independent entrance and its own courtyard and garden in the back.

When they began remodeling, very little of the building's past splendor remained. None of the partition walls was still standing, and only the perimeter walls remained, decorated with old paintings and bits and pieces of former details. This raised the question of how best to divide the interior space. They first thought of curtains, but they finally opted for a few new interior walls, movable wooden furniture, and wooden doors as partitions.

Old floor tiles look like carpets, and seem to repeat the patterns of light and shadows produced beneath the windows. The tiled patches set up directional signals and tensions within the rooms. Everywhere, original patches of fresco remain, along with original ceiling beams and decorations, and gothic arches discovered during construction in the living room. These details and the floor pavings, combined with the contemporary furnishings, lend a patchwork look to the interiors.

A large oak table placed in the hall acts as an indirect model of the house. Made of detachable segments that predict and echo the possible movements of people inside the house, the table is meant as its metaphor. Pieces of this migratory table can often be seen in different rooms, fulfilling various functions.

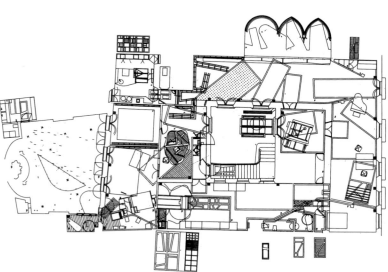

Top: The entryway in the interior courtyard.

Above: General plan showing furnishings and paving.

Opposite: A detail showing the pavings and the recovery of part of the original building. Doorways lead to the study area and the main living room in the background.

Above: Detail of an inter-
mediate space.

Right: A work and study
area.

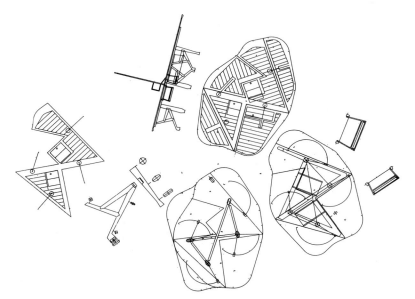

Left: In the foreground, the *Ines-table* designed by Miralles, which divides into smaller tables (see plans, top).

Above, from top: A detail of the shelving designed by the architect; a view toward the door.

Page 126: A work area, with restored
original frescoes on the walls.

Page 127: The living area. The Gothic
arches were discovered during construction and are now being restored.

Right & below: Two views of the kitchen,
including part of the *Ines-table.*

Below: The main bedroom and the half-height partition separating it from the bathroom.

Opposite: The main bathroom, with the bedroom to the left.

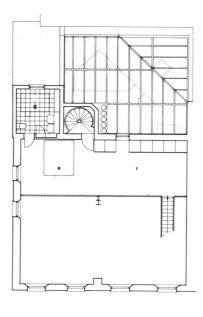

Richard Rogers

London, England 1987

For his own dwelling, Richard Rogers renovated two five-story terrace houses built in 1840 on London's Royal Avenue. Located on a corner site overlooking Sir Christopher Wren's 1692 Royal Hospital and King's Road, both properties were grade II historic buildings and had small, dark gardens to the rear which were devoid of sunlight due to the encroachment of the surrounding buildings.

Rogers divided his house horizontally into four living areas. The older children and their nanny live in three small apartments below ground-level. The ground floor is designed to accommodate the architect's mother-in-law, while the Rogers couple lives primarily on the second and third floors. The fourth floor is reserved for the younger children, and also contains the study area.

The party wall between the two houses was replaced by an open steel support system on the second, third, and fourth floors. In the back of the house, the second floor was partially removed and the original dark courtyard was glassed in to form a three-story entry hall with a narrow mezzanine at the top. A step up from that level is the open living area of the house, with the kitchen on the main floor, and the bedroom and bathroom on another mezzanine above the main floor. The kitchen, with its stainless steel island and small, bright garden terrace, is a central feature of the space. Behind the kitchen, a spiral staircase connects all five floors, bypassing the main living area and its mezzanine.

Rogers ingeniously devised various space dividers to visually separate areas of the large volumes that fill the house. Sliding translucent glass screens divide the living area from the glazed conservatory; venetian blinds conceal the bedroom on the mezzanine from the living area and kitchen below; and on the top floor the large children's room can be divided by an aluminum garage door.

Top: Second and third floor plans.

Left: The main facade illuminated.

Opposite: The double-height living room with armchairs by Le Corbusier, table by Mies van der Rohe, and art by Andy Warhol.

View of the open space, showing kitchen, living room, and stairs.

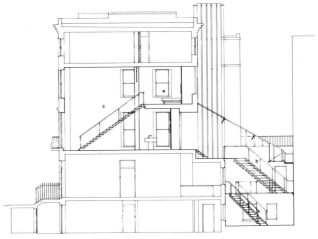

Left: Detail of the back stairs with a painting by Philip Guston on the upper floor.

Above: Longitudinal section.

Below & opposite: The kitchen was conceived as a great metallic island—functional, clean, and easy to maintain

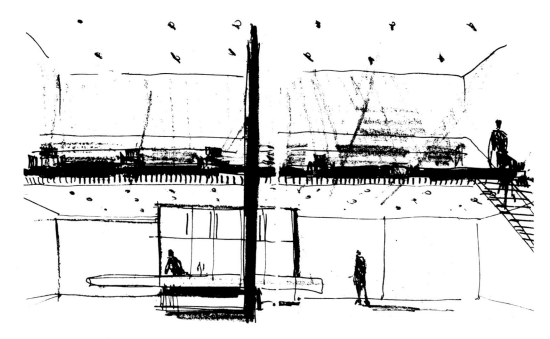

Ettore Sottsass

Milan, Italy 1976

sottsass

Ettore Sottsass is known internationally for his architectural, industrial, and furniture design, ceramics, jewelry, crafts, graphic design, and photography. It is surprising, given his designs for Memphis, which he founded in 1981, that he conceives of architecture neither metaphorically, nor as sculpture, nor monument. For Sottsass, architecture is not object, but volume. The space takes shape as an aggregate of volumes, each with mass, color, materials. He has no interest in weightless architecture.

Located in the old center of Milan on the fourth floor of a palazzo near the Pinacoteca di Brera, Sottsass's Milan apartment is a protective space, a space for existence, defined by his own life within it. His design aesthetic is evident in the objects and details contained in the rooms. A vase designed for Memphis rests on a shelf that echoes its shapes. Some of the casework is faced in Sottsass's own laminate designs. Vibrant colors punctuate the space, which, even with spare, modern furniture shapes, white walls, and light two-tone wood flooring, remains comfortable, flexible, and personal. Guests are required to stop in the small hallway to remove their shoes, a tradition borrowed from the Japanese culture which makes visitors feel at ease and at home.

Like Gae Aulenti's apartment, also in Milan, Sottsass's home is designed as a container where accumulated objects and experiences are kept. The apartment walls are entrusted with safeguarding intimacy while keeping remembrances alive.

Left: Detail of the bookcase.

Opposite: Reception hall of the architect's house with a wall sconce and a vase in the purest Memphis style.

Below & right: The living and dining room furnished with a number of Sottsass' own designs.

The living room, bedroom, and bathroom.

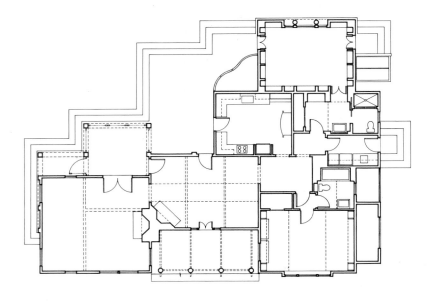

Robert A. M. Stern

East Hampton, New York 1989–91

Since the 1970s, Robert Stern has designed several of the best-known houses in East Hampton, a resort community on Long Island three hours from New York City. For his own summer home there, it would have been easy to design a new house, but Stern chose instead to remodel a pre-existing structure. He bought a typical post-World War II suburban house in a typical suburban neighborhood and set to work to transform it into a gracious and charming country villa.

In the renovations, Stern has used the classical language of architecture in varying degrees of literalness to organize the volumes and give them scale. In his first renovation this language was abstract. Inside, dados and cornices were defined by the most minimal of moldings, and columns were two-dimensional cutouts. In Stern's most recent addition of a master-bedroom suite, the work of two early-nineteenth-century classicists was used as the inspiration. The thick-walled architecture of the suite accommodates books and artifacts in a spatially complex way, modeled after the library at Sir John Soane's house in London. The furniture is designed by Stern himself in the neoclassical style. Outside the room, there is a classical pavilion that faces the garden with a facade inspired by the dining room of Thomas Jefferson's Monticello in Virginia. In his house, Stern carries on the traditional shingle-style facade used in many New England seaside structures, using this same style for other commissioned houses in Montauk, East Hampton, and Quogue on Long Island, and on Fishers Island, Martha's Vineyard, and Marblehead.

Stern has already planned future additions to his cottage home, such as a new living room contained within a shingled tower, which, paired with an existing wing, will bracket the pergola and create a balanced facade to the facing hedged garden.

Top: Site plan.

Bottom: Floorplan.

Opposite top: View of a terrace.

Opposite bottom: The bedroom facade.

Above & opposite: The master bedroom with built-in shelving and a view to the lawn.

Stanley Tigerman

Lakeside, Michigan 1983

Located in a small town in southern Michigan, this one-thousand-square-foot cottage was designed by architects Stanley Tigerman and Margaret McCurry as a family weekend home. The site accommodates an entrance gateway and a raised walkway over the lawn, the house with its attached screened porch, and a pumphouse in the woods. The materials include corrugated sheet-metal siding, marine plywood faced in lattice, and silo roofing. Purposefully vernacular, the main structure with its collection of outbuildings can be seen as the archetypal farm with barn, shed, and granary; and as a church with basilica, narthex, and adjoining baptistry. The lattice facing on the house and the cross-bracing of the walkway railing and porch, however, give the complex a much lighter appearance than the massive forms suggested by these metaphors. Inside, the lattice pattern is repeated on the living room furniture units. At each end of the double-height room, steep stairs ascend to sleeping lofts, while beneath them are an enclosed kitchen and bath at one end, and the master bedroom at the other. In spite of its industrial materials and metaphoric functions, the house has a structural simplicity and handcrafted quality that integrate it with the surrounding countryside and invite informal relaxation.

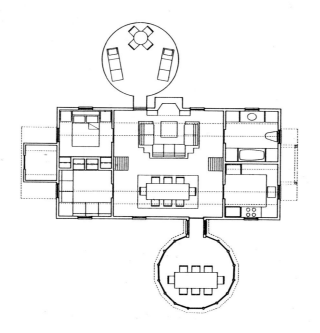

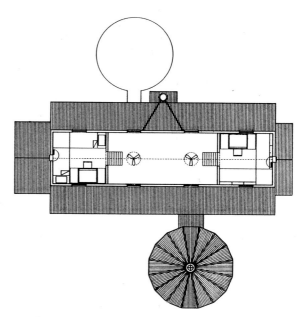

Opposite page: Ground floor and second floor plans.

Left: View from the raised walkway toward the house.

Top: The metaphoric barn and silo.

Above: The entrance gateway.

Above: Dining room.

Right: View from one loft to the other, showing the living room, master bedroom, and study.

The living area.

Bernard Tschumi

New York, New York 1988

For his residence in Manhattan, Swiss-born architect Bernard Tschumi converted an open one hundred thirty-by-thirty-three-foot industrial loft space into a residential apartment. The unusual orientation of the long rectangular space with all the windows on the long sides, as opposed to the more usual configuration with windows on the narrow sides, prompted Tschumi to keep the perimeter walls free from partitioning. A freestanding box-like volume containing bedrooms, bathrooms, and a kitchen was then created in such a way that no new solid wall touches the perimeter walls. This freestanding, but enclosed volume stands within a large living, dining, and reading area, which is defined at each end by black metal library shelving units and partitions made of glass and black anodized aluminum.

The rigorously simple spatial concept used by this dean of the Columbia University Graduate School of Architecture creates three independent parallel bands, each with its own purpose and its own logic. From south to north there is a living, dining, reading, writing, and designing area, followed by the freestanding service core (kitchen, bathrooms, and bedrooms with sliding glass doors), and finally, a hallway which is used as a gallery for artwork.

The loft floor is covered in continuous ebony-stained oak, except for the bathrooms, which are black ceramic tile. The modern steel-tubing furniture, upholstered in black, enforces the sleek functional look of this industrial redesign.

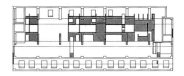

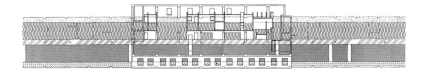

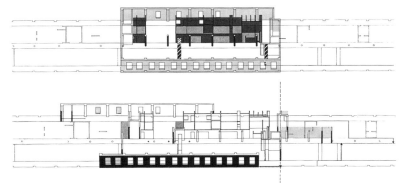

Opposite page: The gallery corridor.

Top & bottom: Volumetric plans showing the central volume, the parallel bands, and the layout of spaces.

Left: The dining room, living room, and library exist in a single open space.

Below: The apartment consists of a series of parallel zones.

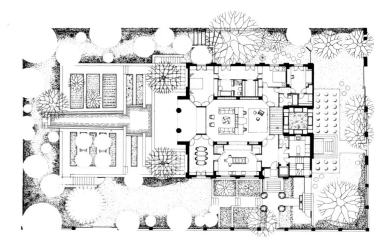

Oscar Tusquets

Barcelona, Spain 1992

Designer, architect, and painter Oscar Tusquets wanted to have a garden inside the city of Barcelona, but with land prices well over the budget he had decided for his home, he considered moving his office into the same building as his home. This measure taken, the opportunity of designing his own home became a reality. Tusquets called the house Villa Andrea in homage to Palladio and in tribute to his own daughter Andrea.

The complex program includes several studio spaces as well as his home, with each part both functional and private. Tusquets's desire to have a garden compelled him to keep the ground floor for himself, while the remaining three levels (two upper floors plus one underground) became his studio. This was built around a two-story central atrium to ease communication among the architects working there.

The symmetrical home interior is organized around a central living space where Tusquets and his family talk, watch TV, read, work, or entertain guests. It is also the space where Tusquets paints, an activity he enjoys immensely. The kitchen was laid out like a professional kitchen for Victoria Tusquets, a well-known chef and former restaurant owner.

The house is filled with Tusquets's own designs for furniture, and his paintings. The mélange of art nouveau-style chairs, Cretan columns, and minimalist bookcases in a Palladian-styled assemblage of spaces is typical of Tusquets's signature postmodernism.

The terraced garden is another element of Tusquets's eclectic mixture of influences. Partly inspired by the gardens at Pompei, it contains a pool and fountain.

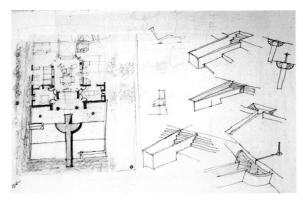

Opposite page, top: Plan of the ground floor and garden.

Opposite page, bottom: The rear facade with the swimming pool in the foreground.

Left: View of the garden and the rear facade.

Top: A detail of the garden.

Above: Preliminary sketches for the pool.

153

Right: Crossection.

Below: Tusquets has furnished his house with a number of his own designs. In the foreground, the Belgravia sofa, Girandola occasional table, and Extra de Varius chairs. The painted trees on the columns are also by Tusquets.

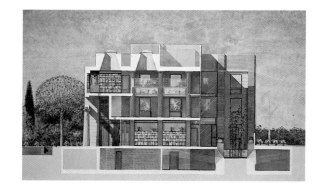

Right & below: Three views of the living room, the central space around which the other rooms are organized.

View of the kitchen with the tea set designed by Tusquets for Alessi.

Left: Looking from the kitchen into the living room.

Below: The dining room.

Below: The master bedroom.

Opposite: The master bath.

Above: Tusquets's double-level studio.

Opposite top: Floor plans of the studio.

Opposite bottom: A general view of the studio, which includes showcases for Tusquets's architectural and object designs.

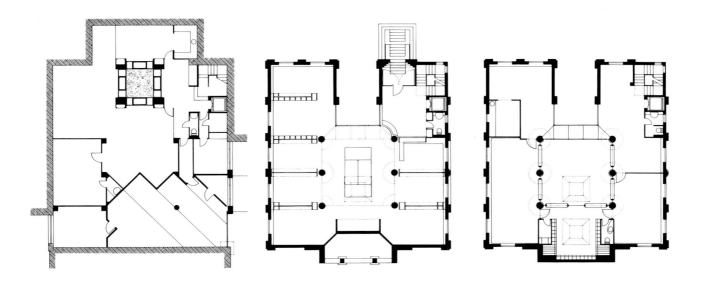

Oswald Mathias Ungers

Utscheid, Germany 1986–88 (Holiday Home)
Cologne, Germany 1959, 1989–90 (Main Residence, Library)

Ungers has a predilection for the simple geometry of the cube. His work is replete with historical references to the Classical Mediterranean tradition whose symmetry and geometry he studies and respects.

Ungers's country home in Utscheid is an autonomous block in a clearing in the woods. Similar in some aspects to the Palladian villas of the Italian Veneto, the residence imposes its volume and presence on a serene landscape surrounded by two natural lakes. The building was originally a glass workshop around the seventeenth century. Later on, it was used as a storage space for agricultural tools. The architectural value of the building is based on the obsessive combination of a single geometric figure: the cube. Every element of the house is either cubic, or a variation on the square. Even the furniture is cubic.

Ungers's private library, which he added on to his main residence in Cologne (1959), echos the cubic form and interior finishes of the summer house in Utsheid, as well as public projects such as his Baden Regional Library in Karlsruhe (1980–92). The library is built of basalt, and receives daylight through four glass cubes set into the roof. The interior is simply a wooden structural skeleton with the bookcases lining the perimeter walls and a spiral staircase uniting the two floors. It is an outstanding library both because of the high quality of its working environment and the rare architectural collection it houses.

The main house in Cologne is built of brick and, with the basalt library, forms an introverted complex in which each element fits perfectly into context. The interior of the main house shows Ungers's reductive cube vocabulary in furniture, art, and space. Ungers and his wife plan to make the Cologne complex the seat of their Ungers Foundation for Architectural Sciences, which will promote architectural learning.

Opposite page, from top: Upper and lower floor plans; the house in its clearing.

Left: The house.

Below left: Looking down the main staircase.

Below: A longitudinal section and a crossection.

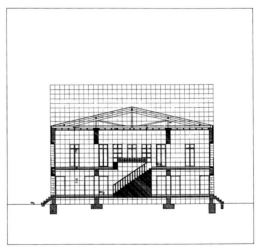

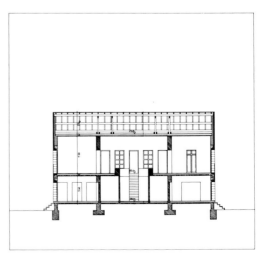

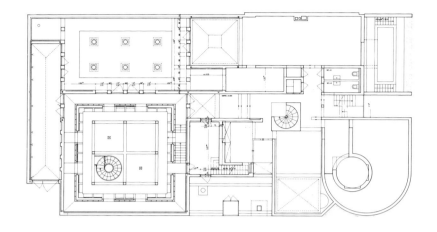

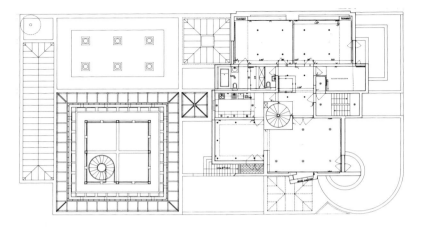

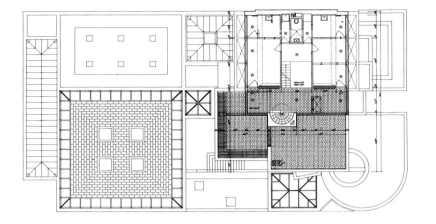

Opposite page, top: First and second floor plans of Ungers's primary residence in Cologne. The cubic library is in the lower left corner.

Opposite page, bottom: The columned courtyard.

Left: Third-floor plan.

Below: The library interior.

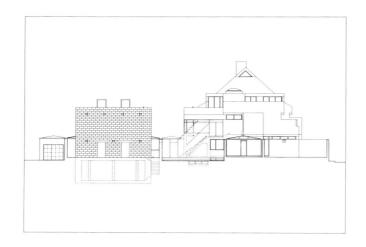

Opposite page, top: Elevation of the main house and library.

Opposite page, bottom: Looking into the living room.

Below: Living room and dining room of the house in Cologne.

Livio Vacchini

Tenero-Contra (Ticino), Switzerland 1992–93

vacchini

Like Aurelio Galfetti, Swiss architect Livio Vacchini is one of the distinguished group of architects based in northern Italy and southern Switzerland. Vacchini's house in Tenero-Contra is a simple, minimal form—a subdivided rectangle. It consists of two parallel, communicating spaces, partially divided from each other by a freestanding partition that holds the kitchen along one wall, and an enclosed bathroom. The surrounding space is open on all sides to a spectacular view of the rural countryside and the mountains across the valley.

The extremely elongated interior space measures about twenty-eight feet in width and about sixty feet in length. In Vacchini's house, the twenty-one-inch-thick, precast, reinforced concrete roof slab rests on three pilasters at either end of the construction. Vacchini used reinforced concrete for the structure, glass, aluminum, and varnished wood for the vertical surfaces, polyurethane for the floors, and plaster for the ceiling. The interior exemplifies Vacchini's typical restraint. While his work is characterized by an absence of historical motifs, his designs seem to abide by Mies van der Rohe's famous proclamation that "God is in the details." The brilliant green-yellow of the interior is one of these details, as are the views from the vast windows. The silent order of Vacchini's house is similar to the static form of Atelier Vacchini in Locarno.

Opposite page, left: Plan.

Opposite page, right: View of the house from the valley.

Below: The house looks out across the valley.

The main door.

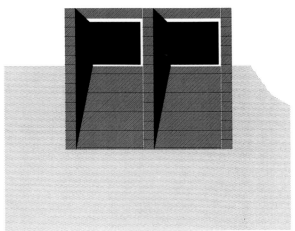

Left: Detail of the pilasters.

Above: Valley-side elevation.

Page 172, top: Side elevation.

Page 172, bottom: The interior. The kitchen is to the right of the single interior wall, with the enclosed bathroom beyond.

Page 173, top: Longitudinal section.

Page 173, bottom: Looking the length of the main room.

171

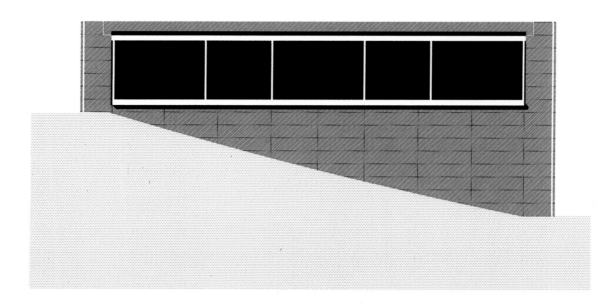

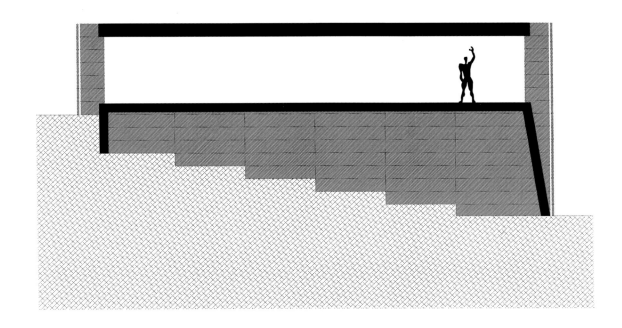

Robert Venturi and Denise Scott Brown

Philadelphia, Pennsylvania, 1983

American architects Robert Venturi and Denise Scott Brown live in one of the very few art nouveau-style houses in the United States. A little-known architect named Milton Medary designed the house in 1909. It sits amidst what was once a rather large estate on the outskirts of Philadelphia, but which was partially subdivided after World War II. As a result, the approach to the house down a long alley bordered by old trees is flanked by "ordinary" suburban homes. What could be more appropriate for Venturi and Scott Brown, who are champions of the ordinary?

Both architects are very interested in furniture and furnishings of all historical periods, and have used the house as a laboratory for working out their own highly eclectic design aesthetic. But even with a Lichtenstein print directly above a Chippendale chair, a Tiffany lamp on a desk next to a neoclassical urn, or faux-Chinese chairs from a demolished Atlantic City hotel in the dining room, everything in the house is compatible—a testament to the critical eye of such renowned designers.

Throughout the house, walls are stenciled in a variety of motifs; in the dining room a freize of honored architects—Lutyens, Le Corbusier, and Loos—are included in the company of Toscanini. Never purists, never classicists, Venturi and Scott Brown confront the variety of tastes and cultures represented in the notion of home.

Right & below: The interiors feature a combination of different details—art nouveau furniture, pop art paintings, popular iconography, country American upholstery.

Opposite: An art nouveau doorway.

Below: The dining room includes a portrait of Elizabeth Taylor by Andy Warhol and a freize featuring names of honored architects.

Opposite: Detail of the dining room.

Shoei Yoh

Itoshima, Fukuoka, Japan 1984–91

The main facade of Shoei Yoh's glass house is suspended on a steep hill, four hundred seventy feet above sea level, providing a panoramic view of the Sea of Japan towards the Korea Strait. During the winter, winds are so severe that the glass facade of the house becomes white, painted with salt. The more fierce the weather is, the more spectacular the view becomes.

On the east side, the house overlooks a small fishing village in the distance, and on the south side there is a swimming pool sandwiched between concrete walls to the east and west. The white marble terrace extends to the north, like a ship's stern, protecting the house from the waves, steering a course between the sea and the sky. Structurally, two vertical concrete slabs suspend the horizontal slabs, defining the house's floor and roof.

Yoh has lived in glass houses for over twenty years. In spite of the tranquility he enjoys in his glass house, he points out that such houses are exposed to the unforgiving severity of the natural environment at the same time as they are inundated with nature's overwhelming beauty. Although he realizes that for some people a safe, sheltered feeling is absolutely necessary, he says that if this condition can be sacrificed, transparent homes provide a closeness to nature that makes one realize one is actually inhabiting it. In this sense, Yoh's is almost a non-existent home—an invisible house that protects its inhabitants while giving the illusion of not being there.

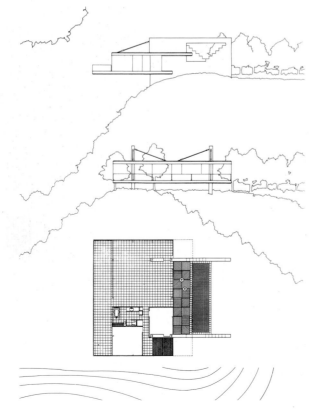

Opposite page, top: The suspended glass house.

Opposite page, bottom: Plan.

Below: The house under the sky.

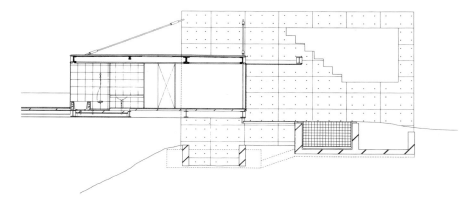

Opposite page, top: Section.

Opposite page, bottom: The terrace looking out to sea.

Left: View from the living room.

Below: The living room and dining room.

Biographies

Stefano Baroni

GAE AULENTI
Born at Udine, Italy in 1927, Aulenti graduated from Milan Polytechnic in 1954. She worked in Ernesto Rogers's studio, with whom she also contributed to *Casabella* magazine. After having worked with Luca Ronconi, Aulenti opened her own office in the early 1970s. Since 1972, when she was included in an exhibition on Italian Design and Architecture organized by the Museum of Modern Art, Aulenti has been in demand as a guest speaker at American universities. Internationally known for her industrial and interior designs, Aulenti has in recent years renovated such cultural landmarks as the Palazzo Grassi in Venice, the Musée d' Orsay in Paris, and the Museu d'Art de Catalunya in Barcelona.

RICARDO BOFILL
Born in Barcelona, Spain in 1939, Bofill studied in Geneva, Switzerland. Upon returning to Spain, he opened his architecture office *Taller de Arquitectura* and designed a series of projects, including Walden 7 and The City in Space, that earned him international recognition. Due to international expansion, Bofill's office started working on large-scale projects and opened branch studios in New York and Paris. Among the architect's latest projects are Catalonia's National Theater in Barcelona, a housing plan in Stockholm, and the 77 W. Wacker office tower in Chicago.

MASSIMO CARMASSI
Born in Pisa, Italy in 1943, Carmassi graduated from Florence Architectural School in 1969. Since 1991 he has been teaching at Florence Art Academy and is a visiting scholar at the Calabria, Torino, Genoa, and Berlin universities. In 1990 Carmassi started a partnership with Gabriela Ioli, who graduated from Florence Architectural School in 1969. Together, they have developed a particular expertise in restoration projects and interior architecture. They were included in the "Emerging European Architects" exhibition organized by Harvard University in 1988.

Miro Zagnoli

Grant Mudford

ANTONIO CITTERIO
Born in Meda, Italy in 1950, Citterio graduated from Milan Polytechnic and began work both as an architect and as an industrial designer. Several of his first designs were produced by the Italian firm B&B and by the German company Vitra. Citterio worked with Gregotti Associatti in the restoration of the Brea Pinacoteque, and in 1986, he started a partnership with American architect Terry Dwan. They are jointly responsible for all the projects developed by the Citterio-Dwan studio since 1986. Citterio and Dwan designed, among other buildings, the Corrente Building and the headquarters for the Daigo Company, both in Tokyo.

DAVID CHIPPERFIELD
Having graduated from London's Architectural Association, Chipperfield worked in the offices of Richard Rogers and Norman Foster before setting up his own office in 1984. He first received international recognition for a series of small scale projects and commercial interior works. In 1987, he opened an office in Tokyo, where he built Japanese fashion designer Issey Miyake's shops, and other projects. In addition to his professional practice, Chipperfield has taught at such institutions as Harvard University, London's Royal College of Art, and Lausanne Polytechnic.

AURELIO GALFETTI
Born in Lugano, Switzerland in 1936, Galfetti studied architecture at Zurich's Polytechnic. He opened his own office in Lugano in 1960. Until 1978, he collaborated with several other architects, such as Flora Ruchat, Livio Vacchini, Rino Tami, Luigi Snozzi, and Mario Botta. Designer of several apartment buildings in the Ticino region, Galfetti has also taught at the architectural schools of Paris, Lausanne, and Lugano.

FRANK GEHRY
Born in Toronto, Canada in 1929, Gehry studied in the USA, where he opened his own architectural studio in 1962. Besides his own famous residence in Santa Monica, Gehry has designed many buildings with significant symbolic components, such as the Vitra Design Museum in Germany, and the California Aerospace Museum in Los Angeles. Also a furniture designer, Gehry has used the figure of a fish as an elemental icon in many of his lamp, interior, architectural, and furniture designs. Gehry was awarded the Pritzker Prize in 1989.

William Taylor

Eichiro Sakata

MICHAEL GRAVES

Born in Indianapolis, Indiana in 1934, Graves studied at the University of Cincinnati, at Harvard's Graduate School of Design, and at the American Academy in Rome. Since 1962 he has taught at Princeton University in New Jersey. He was a member of the New York Five, together with Eisenman, Hejduk, Meier, and Gwathmey. Later, in the early 1970s, Graves's work began revisiting historic architectural vocabularies and values. In addition to running an architectural practice that has earned him several prizes, including *Progressive Architecture* magazine's award and the American Institute of Architects Award, Graves is a well known industrial and furniture designer. His work is included in museums and art galleries around the world.

HIROSHI HARA

Born in Kawasaki, Japan in 1936, Hara graduated from Tokyo University's architectural school in 1959. He obtained his masters and doctorate in 1964 from the same university, where he later became a professor. In 1970 he established *Atellier* in partnership with several other architects. Hara's work attempts to define the role of architecture in the contemporary world. From space architecture to psychophilosophical research on the role of the house in the city and individual life, Hara's theoretical contributions are just as numerous as his built projects. Among his better-known projects are several single family houses, schools, and the Umeda City Skyscraper in Osaka, Japan, completed in 1993.

NORIHIDE IMAGAWA

Born in Hiroshima, Japan in 1947, Imagawa is an architect and structural engineer. He founded TIS & Partners Co. Ltd. in 1978, and soon afterwards, became its president. In 1993, a new TIS & Partners branch was opened in Manila, the Philippines. Imagawa has created a very light prefabricated structural system that allows for quick construction. He has long been involved in research on prefabricated components, particularly prefabricated wood components, on which he has written several books. Among his architectural works are the Higashi Douri Civic Center, the Mito Regional Library, the University of Shizuila, and the Ishiuchi Museum, all in Japan, as well as several works in Southeast Asia, such as the Skywalk Building in Singapore, and a geothermal plant in Palimpinon, the Philippines.

ARATA ISOZAKI

Born in Oita, Japan in 1931, Isozaki graduated from Tokyo University and began work for Japanese architect Kenzo Tange. Isozaki remained with Tange for ten years, and in 1963 started his own architectural firm, Isozaki & Associates. Isozaki's designs include experimental housing, the Museum of Fine Arts in Gunma, Japan, the Museum of Contemporary Art in Los Angeles, California, and the Palau Sant Jordi (Olympic Sports Palace) in Barcelona, Spain. Among the many prizes Isozaki has received are the Japanese Institute of Architects Annual Award, the RIBA gold medal, and the Spanish FAD Architecture Prize.

TOYO ITO

Born in Japan in 1941, Ito studied architecture in Tokyo. In 1971, he founded the architectural firm URBOT (Urban Robot), and in 1971 renamed the firm in his own name. Winner of several architectural competitions, Ito's main works are single family houses built in Tokyo, as well as restaurants, hotels, museums, and other commercial and corporate buildings.

CARLOS JIMÉNEZ

Born in Costa Rica in 1959, and currently living in the United States, Jiménez has been recognized in several international exhibitions for his use of color and simple geometric combinations. In less than fifteen years, Jiménez has attained a brilliant architectural career, as well as an academic one. He has taught at several American universities and is a frequent contributor to well-known international architecture periodicals.

JOURDA & PERRAUDIN

Françoise-Hélène Jourda and Gilles Perraudin's work investigates the lightweight possibilities of prefabricated components and new materials in building. These French architects have called their research Bio-Technology, since it investigates the relationship between architecture and nature, construction and context. They emphasize the active components in architecture, those able to perform a double function. Among their main projects are the Architectural School in Lyon, France, and several apartment buildings, single-family homes, and experimental housing groups. They are both professors at the architectural schools of Lyon, and Oslo, Norway.

RICARDO LEGORRETA

Born in Mexico, where he also studied architecture, Legorreta started his own architectural firm there in 1963. In 1977, he opened a second office in Los Angeles, California, to specialize in home and office furniture. In 1985 he established Legorreta Arquitectos in Los Angeles. Among his many projects are the Camino Real Hotel in Mexico, and several museums, libraries, research centers, and urban planning projects in the United States and Mexico.

Anna Rouker

Luca Vigelli

GEORGES MAURIOS

Maurios studied at the École des Beaux Arts in Paris and worked for Le Corbusier in Chandigarh. He later studied at Harvard's Graduate School of Design, and upon his return to Paris in 1960, he started his own architectural firm. Maurios is extremely interested in industrial prefabrication, and has worked on several experimental housing projects and modular and interactive buildings (buildings that can be transformed by their inhabitants). Maurios has designed several neutral and non-ornamental schools and cultural centers that volumetrically respect the contexts in which they are built.

THOM MAYNE (MORPHOSIS)

Thom Mayne studied at Harvard's Graduate School of Design and at the American Academy in Rome. He has taught in universities throughout the United States, including Harvard, Columbia, Washington University in Saint Louis, UCLA, The University of Texas in Austin, and Yale University. Mayne leads Morphosis, of one of the most innovative architectural groups in the United States. Based in Los Angeles, Morphosis has been experimenting with construction materials, space, and building techniques in a very personal and daring way. Other members of Morphosis are architects Mark MacVay, John Enright, Blythe Alison, Kim Groves, Janet Sager, and Eui-Sung Yi.

MECANOO

The Dutch architectural firm Mecanoo includes Henk Doll and Chris de Wijer, in addition to Erick van Egeraat and Francine Houben, the owners of the house included in this book. They have designed a series of social housing projects and several experimental housing prototypes and have been involved in retail and office design and urban planning. Among their large-scale projects are two buildings on the Dutch University campus.

RICHARD MEIER

Having graduated from Cornell University, Meier established his own architectural firm in New York City in 1963. In 1984, Meier was awarded the Pritzker Prize, perhaps the most coveted architectural award. His architectural works include exhibition spaces such as the Museum of Decorative Arts in Frankfurt, Germany, the High Museum of Art in Atlanta, Georgia, and the Museum of Modern Art in Barcelona, Spain. Meier has also designed cultural centers and corporate buildings in The Hague, Ulm, Munich, Los Angeles, Luxemburg, and other cities.

Seiji Osukima

Barbra Walz

ENRIC MIRALLES and BENEDETTA TAGLIABUE
Born in Barcelona, Spain in 1955, Miralles graduated from Barcelona's architectural school in 1978. He teaches there, and at universities throughout the world, including Harvard University, Columbia, and Princeton. Considered one of the most outstanding architects of Spain's contemporary architectural scene, Miralles has taken a personal approach in his designs for stadiums, schools, cultural centers, a cemetery, parks, and piazzas that has earned him international recognition. Benedetta Tagliabue studied architecture in Venice and worked on her doctorate in architecture in New York, where she also completed several rehabilitation projects. Since 1990, she has lived in Barcelona, where she has worked with several architects and is finishing her doctoral dissertation. She contributes to numerous international architecture periodicals.

RICHARD ROGERS
Rogers graduated from London's Architectural Association and later studied at Yale University. During the 1960s, he was a founder of the so-called Team Four, of which Norman Foster was another member. In the early 1970s, he started his own firm in association with John Young, Mike Davies, and Marco Goldsmith, with whom he designed a wide variety of projects—from industrial buildings, cultural centers, and airports to corporate office buildings and urban masterplanning jobs. Among Rogers's best known projects are the Pompidou Center he designed with Renzo Piano, Lloyd's of London, and urban plans for Japan, South East Asia, and Majorca in Spain.

ETTORE SOTTSASS
Born in Insbruck, Austria in 1917, Sottsass became an architect in 1939. He is best known as one of the founders of the Italian Memphis design group. Memphis was a team of designers and architects who, tired of the functional dogmas established by the Bauhaus, proposed a new language that made use of the expressive components of materials, shapes, and colors. As an industrial designer, Sottsass created the Valentine typewriter, produced by Olivetti and exhibited among selected industrial design pieces at the Museum of Modern Art. Sottsass's work as architect and designer has been shown in exhibitions throughout the world. In 1980, he founded Sottsass Associatti together with Mario Zanini and Aldo Civic.

ROBERT A.M. STERN
Robert Stern studied architecture at Columbia and Yale universities. He has taught at Columbia and has written several books including *Modern Classicism, New Directions in American Architecture,* and *New York, 1900,* followed by 1930 and 1960. Robert Stern is President of an architectural firm with more than 60 employees. They have designed many domestic residences, as well as company headquarters, university campus buildings, and several corporate buildings for the Walt Disney Corporation.

Leopoldo Pomés

Heinz-Günter Mabusch

STANLEY TIGERMAN

Tigerman graduated from Yale University, where he now teaches. A main exponent of postmodernism in America, Tigerman's works can also be found in Italy, Canada, Japan, Portugal, Germany, Bangladesh, Great Britain, and Spain. His designs have evolved through the years to incorporate his research on architectural expression and significance. He has written several architecture books, including *The Chicago Tribune Tower Competition and Late Entries, Versus: An American Architect's Alternatives,* and *The Architecture of Exile.* He often works with his architect wife Margaret McCurry.

BERNARD TSCHUMI

Born in Switzerland in 1944, Tschumi has dedicated most of his professional career to teaching architecture. He has taught at the Architectural Association in London, at Princeton, Yale, and Cooper Union in New York. Since 1988, Tschumi has been Dean of the School of Architecture and Planning at Columbia University. His best-known built architectural project is the Parc de la Vilette in Paris, for which he competed with 470 other architectural teams.

OSCAR TUSQUETS BLANCA

An architect by training, a designer by vocation, and a painter by inclination, Oscar Tusquets (b. Barcelona, 1942) graduated from Barcelona's school of architecture in 1965. He later founded the partnership 'Studio Per' and the product design company BD- *Ediciones de Diseño.* Until 1984, he was associated with architect Luis Clotet, and in 1987 Tusquets started the new partnership Tusquets, Díaz y Asociados, where Carlos Díaz is project manager. Tusquets has built in Spain and several other European and Asian countries, but is best known for his furniture and industrial designs.

OSWALD MATHIAS UNGERS

Born in Kaisesesch, Germany in 1926, Ungers worked in his own architecture studio in Kohl before entering the academic world. As a professor, Ungers has taught in several universities around the world, including Cornell, Harvard, Berlin, Vienna, UCLA, Dusseldorf, and San Luca di Roma. In 1971, Ungers became a member of the American Institute of Architects. His work has been shown in several Architectural Biennial and Documenta exhibits. Ungers's work is considered an excellent example of contemporary German institutional architecture. Among his best-known projects are museums at Kohl, Berlin, Bremen, and Frankfurt.

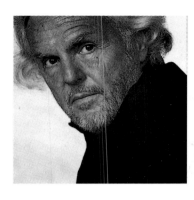

J.T. Miller

LIVIO VACCHINI
Born in Locarno,
Switzerland in 1933,
Vacchini studied architecture in Switzerland and
worked in Paris and
Stockholm for a year. In
1962, he started his architectural career in association with Luiggi Snozzi,
with whom he remained
until 1968. Later, Vacchini
collaborated with Aurelio
Galfetti. Vacchini has won
competitions for hospitals,
industrial buildings, multi-
use spaces, post offices,
cultural centers, sports
halls, and university facili-
ties. He has taught at the
Zurich and Milan polytechnic schools.

**ROBERT VENTURI and
DENISE SCOTT BROWN**
Born in Philadelphia,
Pennsylvania in 1925,
Venturi started his own
architetural firm in 1964,
having worked with Louis
Kahn and Eero Saarinen.
In 1967, Denise Scott
Brown joined the partner-
ship that later was to
become Venturi, Scott
Brown and Associates,
with over 50 employees.
Robert Venturi, as the lead
designer in the firm, was
awarded the Pritzker Prize
in 1991. In their work,
Venturi and Scott Brown
aim to recover the archi-
tectural symbols and mon-
umentality they believe
has been lost in modern
architecture.

SHOEI YOH
Born in Kumamoto, Japan,
Yoh studied economics in
Tokyo and art and archi-
tecture at the Wittenberg
University, in Ohio. In
1970, he established his
architectural firm in
Fukuoka, and in 1992, he
was invited to teach at
Columbia University.
Among Yoh's prizewin-
ning projects are domestic
works as well as commer-
cial spaces and golf cours-
es. Yoh is particularly fond
of glass as a construction
element.

PHOTOGRAPHERS

Satoshi Asakawa, 180–183
Gert von Bassewitz, 42–49
Reiner Blunck, 50–55
Tom Bonner, 109
Richard Bryant/Arcaid, 132–137
Santi Caleca, 18–23, 37–41, 138–145
Mario Ciampi, 30–35
Stéphane Couturier, 98–99
Jean-Pierre Estrampes, 102–107
Georges Fessy, 96–97
John M. Hall, 142–145
Hedrich-Blessing, 147–149
Paul Hester, 90–95
Shigeru Hirabayashi, 81–85
Dieter Leistner/Architekturphoto, 162–165
Lourdes Legorreta, 101 (upper right)
Peter Mauss/Esto, 150–151
Ryuji Miyamoto, 68–71
Grant Mudford, 56–63
Tomio Ohashi, 87
Daria Scagliola, 110–117
Shinkenchiku, 86
Julius Shulman, 100–101
Ezra Stoller/Esto, 118–121
Rafael Vargas, 24–29, 122–131, 152–161
Paul Warchol, 64–67, 174–179
Alo Zanetta, 168–173, cover photo